Nations and Peoples

Mexico

MEXICO

ROBERT MARETT

with 30 illustrations and a map

WALKER AND COMPANY

NEW YORK

Dedicated to José and Aurora

with affectionate gratitude

© Thames and Hudson Ltd. 1971

All rights reserved. No portion of this work may be
reproduced without permission except for brief passages
for the purpose of review.

Library of Congress Catalog Card Number: 72–142855

ISBN: 0–8027–2124–9

First published in the United States of America in 1971
by the Walker Publishing Company, Inc.

Printed and bound in Great Britain

Contents

Preface   *Page* 7

1   Introduction to Mexico   9

2   Tour d'horizon   13

    Map of Mexico   22–3

    plates 1–15   33

3   The Indian heritage   41

4   The legacy of Spain   53

5   The young republic   66

6   The Porfirian dictatorship   82

7   The Mexican Revolution   95

    plates 16–30   121

8   Society in transition   129

9   The people and politics   146

10 The intellectual and social climate   158

11 Mexico in the modern world   169

    Notes on the text   181

    Acknowledgments   185

    Select bibliography   187

    Who's Who   191

    Index   201

Preface

THIS BOOK is a labour of love. Having lived in Mexico for ten years as a young man, and written about the country as it was at the climax of the Revolution under President Cárdenas, it was a fascinating experience to return to Mexico thirty years later and see all the tremendous progress that has been made. It was almost like visiting another country.

I am indebted to Señor Adolfo de la Huerta of the Mexican Tourist Department, who offered me every kind facility; also to many Mexican friends who, whether they realized it or not, helped me greatly simply by speaking frankly about the problems of their country.

As for British friends, I owe a special debt of gratitude to Peter Hope, the British Ambassador, and his staff; the local representatives of the British Council; Stephen Clissold and David Huelin in London; and Mrs Hollman in Jersey for invaluable secretarial assistance.

R.M.

Jersey 1970.

1 Introduction to Mexico

EVER SINCE THE SIXTEENTH CENTURY, when the first glowing accounts of the Spanish *conquistadores* began to trickle back to an amazed Europe, Mexico has had a powerful attraction for foreigners. Explorers, missionaries, archeologists, historians, sociologists, artists, students, businessmen, even football fans – men and women in every walk of life have felt the pull of the Mexican magnet. Nor does one have to be a specialist in any particular field to fall under the spell of this fascinating country. Thanks to modern means of transportation, thousands upon thousands of tourists descend upon Mexico every year, if only in search of the sun and the stimulation of something new. A country of rich diversity, Mexico has something to satisfy almost every kind of taste.

For the lover of natural beauty Mexico offers an unequalled variety of scenery – mountains, jungles, deserts, lakes and tropical beaches; every kind of climate and vegetation; the wildest and most forbidding country imaginable, and then suddenly, just over the brow of the hill, some tranquil valley with its carefully tended fields, peaceful villages and flowering gardens. In truth, as one American writer put it – he used the phrase as the title of his book[1] – there are many Mexicos, from which the traveller can take his pick.   ·

The Mexican countryside is not only scenic, but full of historical associations, for few countries have had a more romantic history than Mexico: a series of remarkable Indian civilizations, the earliest dating from before the time of Christ, culminating, in the sixteenth century, in the bloodthirsty empire of the Aztecs; the incredible feat of the Spanish conquest by 'stout Cortez' and his small band of hardy adventurers; the pomp and glitter of the vice-regal court when 'New Spain' shone as one of the brightest jewels in the Spanish crown;
[1]For references, see p.181.

9

Father Hidalgo's famous battle-cry, 'Death to the Spaniards'; the trials and tribulations of the young republic; the tragic fate of the Emperor Maximilian; the long dictatorship of Porfirio Díaz; and in modern times the unfolding drama of the Mexican Revolution.

It is not possible to travel very far in Mexico without feeling the excitement of a country which is so evidently on the march. On the one hand, reminding one of the past, there are the ruins of ancient Indian cities; primitive Indian villages with their colourful markets and *fiestas*; lovely old Spanish-colonial churches, monasteries and palaces; the archaic ritual of the bull-fight; or merely the evening *paseo* in the plaza of the country town, the men ogling the girls who pass by in giggling groups – one might be back in any small provincial town in Spain. On the other hand, pointing to the future, there is the glittering modernity of Mexico City, a capital of eight million inhabitants, with its skyscraper office blocks, expensive hotels and restaurants, roaring traffic, luxurious residential suburbs, a growing array of factories, and, the most modern touch of all, the newly opened 'Metro'. In art the new 'revolutionary' Mexico first found its expression in the powerful frescoes of Diego Rivera and Siqueiros, but these, with their Marxist emphasis on the social struggle, have already become dated; they do not reflect the *ethos* of the new generation of Mexican revolutionary leaders. A great emphasis on the future, as expressed in the ultra-modern architecture of the National University (which will be familiar to television viewers of the Olympic Games), is probably more representative of the contemporary mood.

Nor is it only in the capital that modernity is challenging the past. In most of the larger cities of Mexico the domes of Baroque churches are being dwarfed by multi-storied blocks of flats and offices; factories are increasingly invading the countryside; and, beyond their range, the countryside itself is no longer immune from inevitable progress. In some places the baronial nineteenth-century country houses, in which the land-owning oligarchy enjoyed the good life before their *haciendas* were seized by the peasants during the Revolution, have been converted into luxury hotels. Quiet little ports, like Acapulco forty years ago, are now lush and expensive seaside resorts. Huge pylons carry electric power over plain and mountain in backward country areas where until recently the villagers were using oil lamps. The most modern farms, employing all the latest equipment and techniques, adjoin smallholdings cultivated by hand tools in the traditional Indian way. Meanwhile a network of modern motor highways, with their petrol stations and motels, has been superimposed upon the map of Mexico.

But there are still, thank goodness, plenty of empty spaces left. Footpaths and mule tracks wind away from the highways on mysterious journeys to who knows where. Beyond those distant mountains – and in Mexico there is almost always a range of mountains on the horizon – the way of life of the people in all probability will not be very much different in its essentials from what it was in colonial times. In these sharp contrasts – and more particularly in the feeling that there is still unknown country to be discovered – lies a great deal of the charm of Mexico. So speaks a foreigner; but it is on the modern aspects of their country that Mexicans prefer to dwell. Thus the foreign author, who ventures to write a book about Mexico, should try not to let his enthusiasm for the antique and the picturesque run away with him. He must steer a middle course between the old and the new, the past and the present. If he dwells on the past, as he is bound to do, it should be primarily in order to understand better the problems of the present.

The purpose of this book is to provide in compact form the essential facts – geographical, historical, economic, social and political – for an understanding of modern Mexico. While its roots go deep into the past, the story which will be told only really begins in the sixteenth century, with the forced imposition of Spanish civilization upon the aboriginal Indian culture. Essentially its theme is the painful process of racial, cultural and economic integration that has been going on ever since between two peoples and cultures of totally different character, resulting at length in the emergence of a distinctive Mexican nation and way of life, which is neither Indian nor Spanish, but derives much from the two parent stocks.

It is a success story, in the main, or so I believe it to be. Since independence in 1821, but more particularly in the last thirty or forty years, Mexico has made enormous strides forward. Economically, the progress of the country has been truly phenomenal – an encouraging example for all developing countries approaching the 'take-off' stage of development. Socially the traditional 'white' oligarchy of the nineteenth and early twentieth centuries, such as still survives in some Latin American countries, has been replaced by a much more broadly based, mostly Mestizo,* middle class. While there are still wide differences between the social classes, in particular between the standards of life of the peasants and the urban population, the problem of racial integration is very nearly solved – there is virtually no racial discrimination in Mexico. Politically, having had bitter experience of both anarchy and dictatorship, Mexico has devised her own unique system of a 'one-party' government, which, while it may not be ideal in theory, succeeds in a rough and ready manner in securing the most essential benefits of democracy while providing – and this is essential in Latin America – for strong centralized government. Most important of all, Mexico has developed a healthy sense of her own national identity. In the nineteenth century she discarded her colonial past; in the twentieth century she managed to free herself altogether from the domination of foreigners and now both foreigners and foreign capital work in Mexico on strictly Mexican terms. In short, Mexico today is well and truly on her own. The modern Mexican can feel proud of his country and confident about its future, while realizing full well that there are still some formidable problems – social, political and economic – which remain to be solved.

*of mixed Indian and Spanish blood and culture.

2   Tour d'horizon

ONE DOES NOT HAVE TO GO all the way as a determinist to agree that the geography of a country has a profound effect upon its history and its social and economic development. This is certainly so in the case of Mexico. A hard and rugged countryside has produced a tough and resilient people. The broken character of the country, with its formidable barriers of mountain, desert, swamp and jungle, has caused a high degree of regionalism, which in its turn has encouraged a tendency towards anarchy and its antidote in the shape of strong centralized government. With not more than 15 per cent (some would put it nearer 10 per cent) of the land surface potentially usable for agriculture, the problem of food supply is acute; this severe geographical limitation, coupled with rapid population growth, is largely responsible for the tremendous economic gulf between the poor peasants, who just manage to scrape a bare living from the land, and the more comfortably situated inhabitants of the cities. Finally, it is not unreasonable to suppose that Mexico's geographical position on the frontier between the United States of America and Latin America has had an important influence upon the Mexican character, serving to foster the strong feeling of nationalism which is so characteristic of modern Mexico.

In shape the main body, or trunk, of Mexico is an inverted triangle. Its base rests upon the 1,614 miles of frontier, running between the Gulf of Mexico and the Pacific Ocean, which separates Mexico from the USA. Its apex is reached at the Isthmus of Tehuantepec where the distance between the two oceans narrows down to only 140 miles. Two vast and complex mountain ranges, the Eastern and Western Sierra Madre (the latter an extension of the Rockies), run roughly parallel with the coasts, converging to form the tangled confusion of

13

the Southern Sierra Madre as the country narrows. The V-shaped plateau between these mountain ranges, lying almost at sea-level on the frontier with the USA, rises gradually as one travels southwards, reaching altitudes of between 6,000 and 8,000 feet in the latitude of Mexico City. In the north the plateau is mostly flat, but in the south transverse ranges of mountains, many of them volcanic, cut it up into a number of isolated basins or valleys.

Attached to the trunk in the north-west is the pendant arm of Lower California, an elongated peninsula of mostly desert country jutting down into the Pacific and separated from the Mexican mainland by a narrow gulf. In the south, below the slender waist of the Isthmus of Tehuantepec, the country broadens out again into a wide area of tropical country adjoining the borders of Guatemala and British Honduras. Having almost disappeared for a moment in the Isthmus, the mountainous backbone of Mexico, running parallel with the Pacific coast, emerges once more in the Sierra de Chiapas and continues down into Central America. To the south-east the country is mostly low-lying, culminating in the limestone peninsula of Yucatán, which, as though to balance the long arm of Lower California in the northern Pacific, projects boldly into the Gulf of Mexico. The total land area of Mexico is 760,172 square miles, about eight times the size of the United Kingdom or the state of Oregon. But since 90 per cent of the country is wilderness only a very narrow base is left to support the population, estimated today to be 48 million, but which is likely to have risen to at least 60 million by 1975.

Climate in Mexico is the function of three variables – latitude, altitude and rainfall. Mexico lies about half in the northern temperate zone and half in the tropics, the line of the Tropic of Cancer running from just south of Ciudad Victoria on the Gulf coast to just north of Mazatlán on the Pacific. But it would be wrong to assume that the climate automatically gets more tropical as one proceeds southwards. Mexico City, for example, lies well down to the south within the tropics – there is a time of year when at midday the sun is dead overhead – but, thanks to its high altitude (about 7,500 feet) it never really gets hot in the capital; indeed the air can sometimes be quite nippy at night. Thus it is customary to classify the Mexican climate, on the basis of altitude, in three zones: *tierra caliente* (hot country), from sea level up to 1,500 feet, with a mean temperature of 77°–82°F; *tierra templada* (temperate country), 1,500 to 6,000 feet, with temperatures running from 70° to 75°F; *tierra fria* (cold country) in altitudes of 6,000 feet and above, with an average temperature of 65°F.

The descriptions 'hot', 'temperate' and 'cold', which the Spaniards used to describe these three climatic zones, are only very relative terms. For example, Mexico City lies in the so-called 'cold' country, but it has a climate which for most of the time is a good deal sunnier and warmer than that of the French Riviera.

Rainfall, the third variable in the equation, is perhaps the most important of all the climatic factors from an ecological point of view. The trade-winds, sweeping in from the Gulf of Mexico, expend most of their moisture on the low-lying tropical country of the Gulf coast and on the seaward slopes of the Eastern Sierra Madre. The same thing happens on the Pacific coast where in some parts south-west winds bring in rain which mostly falls on the western slopes of the coastal range. From either side only a small amount of rain gets through to the central plateau. Thus large areas in northern Mexico are desert, or semi-desert, but the rainfall, although erratic, tends to improve in the south. For example, in Mexico City there is a dry season from October until March when it practically never rains at all. But in the wet season one can almost set one's watch by the heavy thunderstorm which breaks over the city with torrential rain at 4 p.m. and usually continues for at least a couple of hours. These vagaries of altitude, latitude and rainfall have determined the pattern of human settlement in Mexico.

THE CENTRAL REGION

The heart of Mexico is the great Valley of Mexico, or the Vale of Anahuac as the Indians called it. Situated in the highlands at an altitude of 7,500 feet, its setting is superb in a ring of high mountains, dominated in the east by the two snow-clad volcanoes, Popocatépetl (17,783 feet) and its equally gigantic sister, the triple-peaked Ixtaccíhuatl (the Sleeping Lady). In quite recent times by geological standards the whole valley must have been the scene of tremendous volcanic convulsions, for it is pock-marked by craters, and one part of it was inundated by a huge lava flow which swirled over the cultivated fields of the Indian peasants. On the edge of the flow, in the rocky waste of the Pedregal, there still stands at Cuicuilco an ancient pyramid – the oldest monument in the Valley of Mexico (its date is somewhere between 600 and 100 BC) – which was completely surrounded and partially submerged by the lava. But the volcanoes were dormant by the time the Spaniards arrived.

When Cortés got his first sight of the valley (he marched his army over the saddle between the two highest volcanoes) it must have been an even more wonderful sight than it is today. The surrounding mountains, many of them now bare, were then thickly forested. The great lakes which occupied most of the now dry and salt-scarred floor of the Valley were still brimming with water, and carried a heavy traffic of canoes between the lacustrine Indian city states. Tenochtitlán, the Aztec capital, projected into the lake like a miniature Venice, its flat-roofed houses and gardens built on artificial platforms of wattle and mud, and with canals serving as streets. Three giant causeways – in the words of one of the Spanish chroniclers, 'built solidly of lime and stone, defended by drawbridges and wide enough for twelve horsemen to ride abreast' – led across the water from different parts of the mainland and converged upon the central square of the capital, dominated by the great temple of the War God. Today, avoiding the rushing traffic as it circles the Zócalo in the heart of Mexico City, it needs an effort of the imagination to remember that this fine example of a Spanish square was once the centre of Moctezuma's proud capital. Only a fragment of the base of the great pyramid, in an open building-lot behind the Cathedral, has remained on the site.

Nor is it only the Aztec city that has disappeared. The colonial city, which Cortés built, is also in danger of being so overwhelmed by the huge modern city, into which, in the last thirty or forty years, the capital has grown, that the ordinary citizen is hardly conscious of the older parts. The splendid Zócalo, with its typically Spanish cathedral and the austere presidential palace is fortunately intact and unspoiled; it has been made all the more beautiful at night by modern illumination. In the old University district behind the Zócalo, and in the narrow shopping streets between it and the old-world park of the Alameda, there are still some fine colonial churches, buildings and squares to be seen. But the Paseo de la Reforma, a magnificent tree-lined avenue leading away from the old city centre to the palace and park of Chapultepec, which was once graced by the ornate nineteenth-century residences of the rich, is now dominated by skyscraper hotels and office blocks. Formerly smart residential suburbs, such as Colonia Juárez, have become fashionable shopping centres, like Mayfair in

London. Meanwhile new suburbs, with their flowering shrubs and luxurious houses in the latest architectural styles, have spread out over the great valley in an ever-widening circle. To the west, in the Lomas de Chapultepec, the houses have climbed high up into the foothills to escape the smog. To the south, in the Pedregal, not far from the ultra-modern university, a rich man's suburb has been built on the lava flow, with the most cunning use made of the jumbled rocks to construct gardens and site the expensive picture-windowed houses.

In contrast, not very far away, there has been preserved, like a fly in amber, the once secluded little village of San Angel, with its old Spanish houses and narrow, cobbled streets, although it is now completely surrounded by the advancing tide of the city and its outer ring of factories, blocks of workers' flats and shanty towns. For the capital, it must be remembered, is also the principal industrial centre of the country. It is these startling contrasts which make Mexico City such an exciting, if a somewhat exhausting, place to visit. The three stages in the growth of the city are very nicely symbolized in the recently constructed 'Square of the three Cultures'. Here in the centre of a complex of brand-new skyscraper office buildings the foundations of an ancient Indian temple have been excavated and restored to serve as a centre-piece, with a lovely Baroque church standing in the background. It shows at a glance the three stages of Mexico's evolution as a nation – its ancient Indian past, the Spanish colony, and finally, rising triumphantly to the sky, the multi-storied pinnacles of the modern state into which it has grown.

Like the spokes of a wheel, railways and highways radiate out from the capital, and there are good internal air services, too, serving the more distant cities and tourist spots. In whatever direction one travels from the capital the roads are scenic; for on the Mexican plateau it is impossible to go any distance without having to cross some tremendous mountain range, beyond which will lie another valley, at a higher or lower altitude, which will be quite different in character from the one just left behind.

Take, for example, the road from the capital to Acapulco on the Pacific coast, which is probably the most popular of all the tourist routes. A super-highway, following more or less the path of the colonial 'royal road', climbs the high Ajusco range of mountains to the south of the Valley of Mexico and plunges down through a pine forest to Cuernavaca in the neighbouring Vale of Morelos, several thousand feet lower than Mexico City. Thirty years ago Cuernavaca was a sleepy little colonial town; it is now a sprawling week-end vacation resort. But no amount of urbanization can spoil the beauty of its surroundings or its perfect climate. For people fortunate enough to possess their own villas, or who can afford the luxury hotels, it is still a perfect place in which to escape from the altitude and bustle of the capital. The sub-tropical Vale of Morelos was once the principal sugar bowl of Mexico, but its great landed estates were burnt and ravished by Zapata's revolutionary peasant army during the Revolution in the early 1920's. The countryside is peaceful enough today; but Diego Rivera has recorded in dramatic fashion this mighty convulsion in one of his finest frescoes, in a hall of what was once the palace of Cortés overlooking the main *plaza* of Cuernavaca.

Further on, the highway climbs up another range of mountains to Taxco, a little silver-mining town perched on the side of a hill. The mines are now exhausted, but this gem of a town remains as a thanks-offering to their bounty. Although now a Mecca for tourists, Taxco has preserved much of its eighteenth-century charm, with its steep and narrow streets, its miniature *plaza* and its lovely rose-coloured Churrigueresque church, which was donated to the town by a grateful mine-owner, José de la Borda.

On goes the road in typical Mexican fashion, plunging down into the deep gulley of the fast-flowing Balsas river, then up over another high range of mountains, until finally it reaches the Pacific. Acapulco was the port from which the Spanish galleons, laden with Mexican silver, set sail for the Far East, returning with cargoes of silk and other oriental luxuries. Having degenerated in republican times into a run-down little port, it has suddenly come to life again in recent years as one of the most dramatic luxury seaside resorts in the world. But one does not have to travel very far down the coast in either direction from Acapulco to find hundreds of miles of empty beaches and cliffs in a beautiful tropical setting reminiscent of Treasure Island. Although a major industry, tourism still has almost infinite scope for further development.

Even more dramatic perhaps in its natural scenery is the road which leads in the other direction from the capital to Mexico's principal Atlantic port, Vera Cruz. Another super-highway, the road takes the traveller with lightning speed across the high eastern ridge of the mountains and down into the adjacent valley of Puebla. The old colonial city of Puebla is full of interesting churches and monuments, and it is also now an important centre of industry. But the factories have been built in the surrounding countryside and the centre of the town has preserved much of its Spanish character. It is a delight to sit at a café under the arches in the main square and watch the world go by. Over the way there rises the massive bulk of the cathedral, a superb example of early colonial architecture in the Plateresque style, its towers decorated by yellow and red tiles. Puebla, now one of the most important provincial cities of Mexico, was originally established by the Spaniards for strategic reasons as a halfway house between Vera Cruz and the capital; but the region with its rich valley was important long before that. A few miles away, in the old Indian city of Cholula, a great centre of learning in Toltec and Aztec times, the huge mound of a pyramid, once dedicated to Quetzalcoatl, the feathered serpent, rears itself up from the plain, with a Spanish church perched on its summit as tangible proof for the faithful of the overthrow of the old pagan gods.

If one can tear oneself away from the delights of Puebla the highway continues as straight as a die across the plateau, with farms stretching to the horizon on either side, the land green and luxuriant in the rainy season, but dry as a desert in the winter months. Having reached the eastern edge of the plateau, under the shadow of the mighty Orizaba, the highest snow peak in Mexico, the road suddenly plunges down towards the Gulf of Mexico. This is how a British writer[1] described the scene: '. . . entire climates descend vertically like strata. First, so near-seeming, the snowy rock peaks; then the dark regimental pine forests; then the lower forests, looking greener and more disorderly, streaked with charcoal-burners' blue-smoking pyres here and there; then the upper, cooler maguey plantations or citrus groves and the first outbreaking tropical colours of oleander, bougainvillaea, hibiscus, lilies and the rest; finally the tropical coastal jungle interspersed with brilliant green plantations of sugar, bananas, cocoa. . . . Down, zig-zagging through these climatic strata, stretching 12,000 out of the 18,000 feet and more, runs the highway.' Approaching the base of the mountains the traveller is well advised to stop off in Fortín de las Flores. Living up to its name, gardenia petals float on the surface of the swimming pool of the luxurious hotel. The whole region is a tropical garden, with the coffee plantations covering the steep hillsides under the watchful eye of snow-clad Orizaba.

Vera Cruz is something of an anticlimax. Unlike the tropical exuberance of Acapulco, the coast on this side of Mexico is low and rather barren – just an endless line of sand-dunes broken here and there by a cluster of palms. Although one of the oldest cities in Mexico, there is nothing much of architectural interest to be found in the town, apart from the old Spanish fort of San Juan de Ulúa which guards the entrance to the port. But perhaps just because it is not a tourist resort, Vera Cruz has a certain charm. At night the town comes to life. The polygeneous inhabitants – men, women and even the youngest children – parade through the streets and round the *plaza* in gesticulating groups, or lounge in the pavement cafés under an inky star-spangled sky. Street vendors pursue the small groups of foreign sailors on shore leave. But if life in Vera Cruz is leisurely and carefree as befits the tropics, the port, under the protection of its British-built breakwaters, is usually well filled with shipping. All night long, locomotives can be heard clattering about in the freight yard of the busy terminal of this gateway into Mexico.

The various highways which radiate out from Mexico City in a northerly direction, eventually reaching various points on the US border, are less scenic than those described, but they, and their offshoots, lead to all sorts of interesting places within easy reach of the capital. For example, for the archeologically inclined, a run of less than an hour by car takes one to the majestic ancient city of Teotihuacán, with its mighty pyramids of the Sun and the Moon, and many other fascinating monuments. It was the capital of an unknown and nameless people who ruled the Valley of Mexico in the early centuries of the Christian era. Nearby is the austere, fortress-like monastery of Acolman, a relic of the early days of the colony when the Spanish missionaries, barefooted and living in truly Christian poverty, dedicated their lives to converting the heathen. At Tepozotlán,[2] also a short distance from the capital but on another route, the richly decorated Churrigueresque convent shows what happened to the Roman Catholic Church in Mexico when later it became rich and soft. But despite the luxuriance and flamboyance of the gilded interior of the chapel the final effect is one of beauty; for the Mexicans were superb artists and craftsmen and knew how to create harmony out of a mass of intricate detail.

Finally, for scenery and the picturesque, the road which leads out of Mexico towards the west is probably the most beautiful: high wind-swept Toluca under the shadow of its snow-capped volcano (like Puebla it is now beginning to be surrounded by factories); Morelia, unspoilt by industrialization and with its splendid church; and not far off the mountain-girt lake of Pátzcuaro in which, although the waters are receding, the Tarascan Indians still cast their butterfly nets for fish and use the native spear-thrower (*atl-atl*) to hunt duck. Further afield to the north-west (a full day's drive from the capital) the important city of Guadalajara is the focal centre of the four western states of Colima, Jalisco, Nayarit and Zacatecas in which, especially in Colima, there is some lovely unspoilt country to be found. Founded in 1530, Guadalajara was the second city of the Spanish colony and the administrative centre for a huge untamed area lying to the west and north. It boasts, not only of a football stadium, but also of many fine colonial monuments – the cathedral and countless other churches, the elaborate Churrigueresque Governor's palace, some nice old houses and fountains, and a number of museums. But, as elsewhere in Mexico, modernity intrudes. Guadalajara is now an important industrial centre, with more than one million inhabitants, serving the markets of western Mexico.

The seven major valleys of the central plateau – the Vale of Anahuac containing the capital; the lofty basin of Toluca; the huge fertile basin of Guanajuato, containing that city, Querétaro and Morelia; the basin of Jalisco with the country's second city, Guadalajara; the valley of Puebla, and that of Morelos – are responsible for a considerable proportion of the country's agricultural output; for example, most of the maize, the staple food of the people, is grown in these areas. As one writer put it 'the seven-eighths of the country outside these seven valleys comprise the Mexican problem of poverty'.[3] The metropolis together with its hinterland of eleven states, contains more than half the population of the country and is by far the greatest centre of industry. Both politically and economically it is the core of Mexico.

THE NORTH

Northern Mexico, a huge area of desiccated and sometimes completely desert country comprising the territory of southern Lower California and seven states,[4] is like another world. Between them these northern states cover more than half of the land area of Mexico; but they manage to support only one-fifth of the population. The home of nomad Indians in prehistoric times, this barren area had few attractions

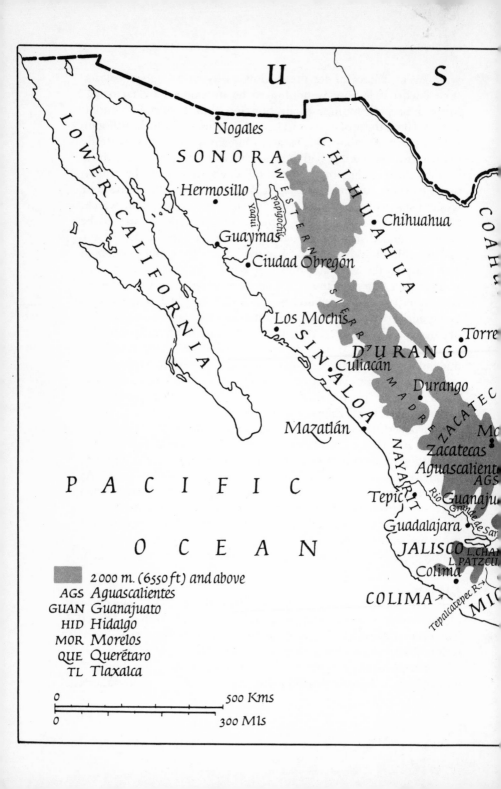

U S

Nogales

SONORA

CHIHUAHUA

COAHU

Hermosillo

Chihuahua

Guaymas

Ciudad Obregón

Los Mochis

Torre

DURANGO

Culiacán

Durango

ZACATEC

Mo

Zacatecas

Mazatlán

Aguascalientes

AGS

PACIFIC

Tepic

Guanaju

Guadalajara

Río Grande de San

OCEAN

JALISCO

L. CHA

L. PATZCU

Colima

Tepalcatepec R.

COLIMA

MI

2000 m. (6550 ft) and above

AGS Aguascalientes
GUAN Guanajuato
HID Hidalgo
MOR Morelos
QUE Querétaro
TL Tlaxalca

0   500 Kms

0   300 Mls

for Spanish settlers; during the time of the colony it was regarded as a buffer between Mexico proper in the south and the English and French settlements in the north. The land is mostly too poor for agriculture – only in favoured spots does irrigation make it possible to grow crops such as cereals and cotton. Much of the area, when not completely desert, is cowboy country, with huge cattle ranches (some of them modern and efficient) extending for hundreds of miles.

In the late nineteenth century the north began to come to life with the development of railways, mining and stock-raising. As the result of North American influences from across the border, industries too were established. Monterrey became a major industrial centre, second only to Mexico City, with its steel mills, brewery and other factories. In the Laguna district, of which Torreón is the centre, the utterly barren alkali desert, one of the harshest in the country, was turned into a flourishing centre of cotton production by irrigation; hundreds of wells were sunk to tap the sub-soil waters. It is a strange experience to approach the Laguna on the road from Monterrey. Driving through this pitiless waste, the surface blinding white under the sun, one experiences curious mirage effects, so that looking ahead one seems to be approaching a lake. Suddenly out of the receding lake on the horizon, a line of trees – and they turn out to be real trees – emerges. As though by magic, the desert comes to an end and one enters a luxuriant countryside. Farmers are working busily on their irrigated plots and the road is blocked by trucks heavily laden with produce for the market.[5]

If the Laguna cotton-growing area represents a late nineteenth-century success story, even greater miracles are being performed today, especially in the north-western corner of the country. For example, in Sinaloa, the El Fuerte reservoir – a veritable inland sea – provides energy for a market-garden area that supplies Mexico's canning industry. There are similar combined hydro-electric and irrigation schemes at Humaya, also in Sinaloa, and at Guadalupe on the river Papigochic near Chihuahua.[6] Thanks to these various efforts the north-western states of Mexico have been transformed out of all recognition during the last twenty years. A tourist entering Mexico by car in the 1950's by way of Nogales in Arizona would have had to take his own food, found very poor, flea-bitten accommodation in the few inns on the way, bumped along over unpaved roads, en-countering here and there a primitive ferry, his car balanced precariously on two canoes hitched together with poles and ropes. Today there are modern highways and luxury motels, with heated swimming pools and a hi-fi radio in every bedroom. Towns such as Hermosillo, Guaymas, Ciudad Obregón, Los Mochis and Culiacán, which used to be poor little places, now give a vivid impression of prosperity, with new buildings rising on every side and clean streets bustling with traffic. For example, forty years ago Ciudad Obregón consisted of nothing but the railway station and a cluster of adobe and wooden shacks. It is now a city of 100,000 inhabitants. This is entirely thanks to irrigation. A dam in the vicinity of the town has enlarged the irrigated land in the valley to 600,000 acres, giving harvests which earn an average of 65 million dollars a year. Producing wheat, cotton, rice, soya beans, vegetables, and sugar cane, the state of Sonora, which was once a desert, is now in second place measured by the value of its agricultural output. Sinaloa occupies the fifth place, with a major production of tomatoes on new irrigated land in the Culiacán Valley. Industries, too, are being developed. In the frontier border towns, which before consisted mainly of brothels and gambling joints, factories, employing Mexican labour, are producing cheap goods for US consumption, to the considerable annoyance of the US authorities. Along the Pacific coast a flourishing shrimp industry is being developed, and, of course, with so many lovely beaches, the possibilities for tourism are unlimited.

In short, the north is developing, although it must be realized that a large part of the northern desert is probably untamable. In this frontier region life is tough, and it has produced a tough breed of men, in many ways more North American than Mexican in their attitude towards life. The successful industrialists of Monterrey are as polished in their dress and manners as any other city-bred Mexicans. But Pancho Villa, with his broad *sombrero* and array of pistols, is the folk hero of the north, and perhaps best expresses its restless spirit.

THE SOUTHERN HIGHLANDS
This is a completely different world, consisting of the southern states of Oaxaca and Guerrero which occupy the base of the V to the north of the Isthmus of Tehuantepec, where the coastal ranges converge to form a complex jumble of mountains; and, south of the Isthmus, the mountainous backbone of the State of Chiapas which continues down to the Guatemalan border. This is essentially Indian country,

as the central plateau used to be until modernity took over. The main towns in this region are Spanish in character, but in the pockets of the mountains small isolated communities of Indians, speaking their own languages and wearing their native dress, pursue their traditional tasks as peasants, with very little contact with the outside world. This region is therefore the happy hunting ground of anthropologists and lovers of the picturesque.

However, this is the poorest part of Mexico, with most of the people, outside the larger towns, living at a bare level of subsistence little different from that which prevailed during colonial times.

Oaxaca, the provincial capital, is one of the most delightful spots in Mexico. With a perfect climate, the town is small enough to allow one to walk to wherever one wants to go, to see the innumerable churches, potter about in the colourful markets or visit the excellent little museum. It has the pleasant slow rhythm of a Spanish provincial town, with the church bells chiming the hours, and its life centred upon the tree-shaded plaza where people, rich and poor alike, loll on the benches or form animated groups in the pavement cafés, to be interrupted every five minutes by itinerant vendors of gorgeously coloured *sarapes* (blankets) and other local wares. When the Indians come to town on market days all is colour, and there will probably be a *fiesta* or procession of some kind. Long-haired foreign hippies in exotic garb mingle with equally long-haired and exotic Indians, and nobody takes any notice (the female hippies are known locally as *hipas*). The surrounding country is magnificent in its scenery and full of interest. The ruined city of Monte Albán, the seat of the Zapotec kings, looks down on the modern city from high up on a mountainside. A good time to visit it is at sunset, when the great courtyard encircled by lofty pyramids is deserted, and the hills in the valley below glow red in the light of the setting sun. The carvings at Monte Albán, depicting Indian dancers, are primitive and grotesque, in contrast with the sophisticated arabesque decorations of the buildings at Milta, another fine archeological site which lies to the south. Or one can just enjoy the countryside, with its oxcarts, primitive little villages and crumbling churches. Oaxaca is that rare combination – a tourist's paradise, yet barely discovered and therefore unspoilt.

Guerrero is wilder and more rugged than Oaxaca. But the bare mountains are full of small pockets of minerals, only waiting to be exploited by any adventurous prospector who is prepared to cope with an almost total lack of communications. As one of my youthful follies I acquired an interest in a silver mine in Guerrero, to reach which it was necessary to float down the fast-flowing Balsas river on a raft, and then on horseback climb up a steep mountainside. The Indian workers were wild-looking creatures with their faces horribly discoloured by a disease called *pinto*. The concentrates from the mine – it really did contain silver – had to be carried on the backs of mules for several days before reaching the nearest railhead. But this was forty years ago. Today at a place called Infernillo (Little Hell) on the lower reaches of the Balsas river, where it joins with the river Tepalcatepec, the waters have been dammed and a huge reservoir is being built which will be twice the size of Mexico's largest lake, Chapala. The electric plant, tunnelled into the mountain and as deep as a twelve-story building, will have 600,000 kW. capacity, and is designed to meet the ever-increasing demands for power in Mexico City and its industrial hinterland.[7]

Lying to the south of these two states, the narrow waist of the Isthmus of Tehuantepec is important to Mexico both strategically and commercially as providing a short land bridge between the Atlantic and Pacific oceans, although perhaps less so today than it was before the Panama Canal was built. A railway constructed at the beginning of the century by British engineers joins the river port of Coatzacoalcos on the Gulf coast with the artificial harbour of Salina Cruz on the Pacific (see below, p. 86). The region is also an important secondary centre of the oil industry, with a refinery at Minatitlán and a number of oilfields hidden away in the depths of the surrounding jungle. While the oil workers sweat and toil, not far away in the little town of Tehuantepec, on the Pacific side of the Isthmus, the male inhabitants are reputed to live in idleness, being content to be dominated and cared for by their splendid-looking women, who are famed for their good looks. On special occasions these Indian beauties show themselves to the world in all the finery of their native dress – embroidered cotton or lace blouses, brightly coloured skirts, elaborate headdresses and a profusion of jewelry.

Below the Isthmus, in the mountain valleys of the Sierra de Chiapas, live some of the most primitive Indians in Mexico. The Presidential candidate, Luis Echeverría, visited this region in February 1970, and some horrifying facts were put before him by the local authorities; 500,000 Indians living in subhuman conditions and bartering their meagre rations of food for alcohol; feudal conditions of work on some of the farms; more than a million people without drinking water; only 1.2 per cent of the land irrigated and assisted by credit; only 64.6 per cent of the inhabitants more than seven years old had been to school.[8] For some years now, in order to try to remedy these conditions, the Mexican government has maintained an Indigenous Institute in the area (see below, p. 134), but it is faced with an uphill task. Irene Nicholson tells how in one Chamula Indian village an ultra-conservative chieftain stubbornly refused a proposal of the Institute that electricity should be installed, arguing that it was against the will of the gods. It was only when a neighbouring village, with a more forward-looking chief, got light, and Indians from afar flocked to see the glittering wonder, that the old man's resistance to modern progress was broken down.

THE TROPICAL LOWLANDS

The *tierra caliente* (hot land) stretches in a great arc from Tampico on the northern part of the Gulf coast, through the State of Vera Cruz, and then broadens out, as the coast curves towards the east, into the vast low-lying tropical expanses of Chiapas, Campeche and Tabasco, ending up in the peninsula of Yucatán and the territory of Quintano Roo. Most of this country is covered by jungle; its principal source of wealth is oil, with important fields in Poza Rica, the Isthmus of Tehuantepec and Tabasco. But most of the people live by agriculture, either working on plantations, or clearing little patches in the jungle for their own use.

Since land communications are poor (although there is now a rail-way and a road running from the Isthmus to Mérida), the best way to form an impression of this region is to see it from the air: there is a daily air service between Mexico City and Mérida, with stops at all the most important towns in between. Better still, make up a small party and charter a light aeroplane in Villa Hermosa, the capital of Tabasco, in order to visit the ruins of the ancient Maya city of Palenque, situated some hundreds of miles inland in the foothills of the Chiapas mountains. For an hour or so the plane flies low over the flat waterlogged country, lying on either side of the winding Usuma-cinta river, which stretches endlessly to the horizon in all directions. The higher ground is covered by huge patches of unbroken jungle. Only an occasional clearing, with its pathetic collection of palm-thatched huts, indicates the presence of man. There are virtually no roads to be seen, most of the traffic being by canoe on the rivers. In short, this is real Graham Greene country, such as he described with such devastating force in *The Power and the Glory*. It is with a feeling of relief that one sights at last the blue line of the Chiapas mountains. As the plane circles down to land on the makeshift airstrip, the ruins can be seen in a clearing on the mountainside, the great temples gleaming white against the dark green of the tropical forest.

Palenque (famous for the exquisite quality of its sculpture) was one of the great cities of the Old Maya empire. This unique civilization flourished in the first centuries of the Christian era and spread over a wide area which included not only the tropical regions of southern Mexico, but vast territories in Central America as well. In ecological terms it represented man's conquest of the tropical forest. A great number of fine ceremonial centres were built, concerning which history is completely silent, although they can be arranged in a rough chronological order on the basis of inscriptions; for the Maya were expert astronomers and developed a calendar and a script. The end of the Old Maya empire is almost as mysterious as its beginning. Perhaps the climate became wetter, making it more difficult to control the forest; or the soil, after frequent burning of the bush for agriculture, became exhausted. Whatever the cause, the rulers of these great cities suddenly abandoned their fine temples and palaces and trekked off elsewhere, some of them to Yucatán, where there was a renaissance of Maya culture. By the time of the Spanish Conquest the jungle had swallowed up all traces of the Old Maya empire, and it was not until the beginning of the nineteenth century that its ruined monuments began to come to light.

Standing there on the summit of the ruined palace of Palenque one realizes what a great change has come over the countryside. When Palenque flourished as a religious and civic centre, the wide plain of Tabasco must have teemed with busy villages, each with its fields of maize in temporary clearings in the jungle. Whatever the cause, there is hardly a sign of civilization now, but it would be wrong to write off this huge expanse of swamp and forest as being useless to man. Mexican experts have recently been carrying out ambitious plans for draining and resettling large areas of this abandoned country. So it may be that the Maya miracle play is about to be reenacted in modern dress.

29

One such major development scheme, first projected in 1951, known as the Plan Chontalpa, has involved massive engineering works in the State of Tabasco designed to control the flood waters of the rivers in a swampy area which suffers from some ten months of heavy rain a year. By this means a huge area of almost useless jungle and swamp has been converted into rich farm land, and a model agrarian community, with schools, social centres and other facilities, is being created. Further north, in the Papaloapan basin in the State of Vera Cruz, a vast hydro-electrical scheme has been undertaken. The catchment area is over twice the size of Wales or Maryland. The plan, which involves a number of government departments, as well as the Indigenous Institute, includes electricity supply, irrigation and the rehabilitation of the Indians of the region. Whether such schemes will ever enable large numbers of landless Indians from the plateau to be settled in the tropics, as some people have dreamed, remains to be seen. The difficulties are formidable in a region with the heaviest rainfall in the world and one which furthermore is ravaged by hurricanes, insects, parasites and tropical diseases.[9]

Yucatán, at the south-eastern limit of Mexico, lies in the tropical rain belt. But, since the peninsula consists of porous limestone, it has no rivers, and the soil is arid unless the sub-surface waters are tapped by means of wells. Mérida, the provincial capital, is a fresh, clean city of mostly flat-roofed, one-story houses, utterly un-Mexican in appearance. It stands in the midst of a flat plain dotted with windmills, with here and there a great plantation of the henequen cactus, the principal industry of the region. The Indians, even in the town, mostly talk the Maya language, with only a smattering of Spanish; and they refer to the Mexicans, that is to say the Mexicans of the plateau, as though they were foreigners. Beyond the range of the henequen plantations, most of Yucatán is covered by dense scrub, and there are few villages. But the whole peninsula is dotted with the ruined cities of the New Maya Empire, of which the great city of Chichén Itzá was the principal centre. Here in this magnificent site one can see the old classic Maya style overlaid by a new style of architecture imported from the Valley of Mexico. Some of the buildings, such as the beautifully restored Temple of the Warriors, are very fine; there is also a good example of a Mexican ball court, and an interesting round tower which was used as an observatory.

But perhaps the most important feature of this city is the sacred well, or *cenote*, into the water of which, so the guides tell one with evident relish, the bodies of sacrificial victims were flung. The priestly rulers of the Old Maya empire were faced by the problem of too much water; the New Maya empire had too little. But in both cases native ingenuity, supported by religion and magic, was equal to the ecological challenge.

In this lightning tour of Mexico a great deal has been left out. But it will have served its purpose if it has brought home to the reader the tremendous variety of scenery, climate and ecological conditions that are to be found, and the many interesting things that are to be seen. Mexico is a tourist's paradise. For the majority of Mexicans (except those who live in the cities and are insulated from the harsh realities of life) the environment is tough; from the very beginning the people of Mexico have had to work hard, often under cruel conditions, in order to scrape a bare living from the soil. Mexico is rich in minerals and oil, and in its different climates it can grow almost every kind of crop. But with less than 10 per cent of the land under cultivation, and with a population which persists in growing along Malthusian lines, there is never enough of the bare essentials of life to go round. Thus merely to keep going is a struggle; to improve the lot of the people in any significant way, as the Mexican Revolution is trying to do, is a task of truly formidable dimensions.

1 *Right:* stucco panel on the palace at Palenque, one of the great cities of the Maya civilization (about AD 800). The two figures are grasping a serpent.

2 The warlike Aztecs were much addicted to human sacrifice. This picture from a fifteenth-century manuscript shows a priest cutting the heart from a living victim on the temple steps.

3, 4 *Above:* the beautifully restored Temple of the Warriors at Chichén Itzá, the principal Maya city of Yucatan. *Below:* the Temple of the feathered serpent god, Quetzalcóatl, at Teotihuacán.

5 Hernan Cortés: bronze medallion of 1529. On Good Friday, 1519, he landed at Vera Cruz with 555 men, burnt his boats, and marched inland to conquer the Aztec empire.
6 The lavishly gilded chapel of the convent of Tepozotlán.

7 On 10 September 1810 the
parish priest Father Miguel
Hidalgo (*right*) preached a
sermon that has come to be
regarded as Mexico's declaration of independence, sparking
off a bloody revolt. His
idealism and sympathy for
the Indians led him to the head
of an uncontrollable army.
He was captured and executed
in 1811.

8 Archduke Maximilian of
Habsburg, placed on the Mexican
throne in 1864 by Napoleon III in
an attempt to protect French
investments in a country torn by
civil war. A well-meaning but
ill-informed prince, he was no
match for the idealistic but ruthless
liberal leader Juárez.

9, 10 After a two-year reign,
Maximilian was driven from his
throne. Defiantly opening his shirt
front, he faced a firing squad of
Juárez's troops together with
royalist generals Mejía and
Miramón. Benito Juárez (*right*)
ruled Mexico as president from 1867
to his death in 1872.

11–14 Four figures from the recent past: Porfirio Díaz (Dictator, 1876–1911), Francisco Madero (President, 1911–13), Venustiano Carranza (President, 1915–20), Alvaro Obregón (President, 1920–24). Only Díaz died a natural death.

15, 16 Pancho Villa (*left*), and
Emiliano Zapata (*above*) are
two of the most colourful of
the revolutionary leaders.
Together they fought against
Huerta and Carranza after
Madero's murder, and
continued guerrilla warfare
until they were both
assassinated, Zapata in 1919,
and Villa in 1923.

17 'Repression', a mural by Diego Rivera in the National Palace, Mexico City. His socialist-realist frescoes tell the story of the Mexican Revolution with the political passion of a convinced Marxist.

3   The Indian heritage

'THE INDIAN BLENDS into the landscape until he is an indistinguish-able part of the white wall against which he leans at twilight, of the dark earth on which he stretches out to rest at midday, of the silence that surrounds him. He disguises his human individuality to such an extent that he finally annihilates it and turns into a stone, a tree, a wall, silence and space.' With these words a Mexican poet[1] described the living descendants of the builders of those lofty temples and richly adorned palaces whose ruins lie scattered about the countryside in such profusion. Who were these mighty builders? What is the significance for modern Mexico of the Indian heritage?

The term 'Indian' is a misnomer when applied to the aboriginal inhabitants of the New World. It stems from the famous mistake of Columbus who, when he made his landfall on the island of Hispaniola in the Caribbean, thought that he had reached the East Indies by the westerly route. But, although not Indians in the sense that Columbus had thought, the native population of the New World is of Asiatic origin. Physical features, such as slightly slanting eyes, a yellow or copper skin, straight dark hair, a sparse beard, indicate that the aboriginal Americans belong to the Mongoloid branch of the human family. It is generally agreed by archeologists that their ancestors must have drifted into the empty continent of America in small hunting groups across what is now the Bering Strait. This migration from the steppes of Asia must have begun towards the end of the last Ice Age, perhaps 25,000 years ago, when there was an ice-free land bridge joining eastern Siberia and Alaska. The exact dates are uncertain. There is, however, irrefutable archeological evidence, based on radio-carbon dating, to prove that, as early as 7000 BC, there were Indians in Mexico – men of the same general physical type as the present-day Indians – who hunted the mammoth; the remains of these giant creatures, together with the stone weapons with which they had been killed, and near by the graves of their hunters, have been unearthed in the Valley of Mexico.

It does not fall within the scope of this book to trace in detail the progress of the Mexican Indians through the various stages of their evolution towards civilization.[2] By about 5000 BC groups of semi-nomadic Indians, still very primitive, subsisting precariously on the edge of the desert in northern Mexico, were cultivating a primitive maize; but it was not until about 1500 BC that agriculture, based on the cultivation of maize, beans and squash, had replaced hunting and food-gathering as the economic basis of society, enabling the Indians to settle down in permanent villages in the more fertile valleys of the highlands and on the tropical flat-lands of the coast. From this early Neolithic, or formative stage, which culminated with the Olmec civilization on the Gulf coast, it was only a short step, on the evolutionary time-scale, to the full flowering of the Indian civilizations of the Classic Period (AD 300–900), as exemplified by the Old Maya Empire in the tropical south, the Zapotec Kingdom of Monte Albán in the Vale of Oaxaca, and, mightiest of all of the city states of this era, Teotihuacán in the Valley of Mexico.

This was the Golden Age of Indian Mexico. On the basis of a technology that was essentially Neolithic, for metals were unknown until after AD 900, the Mexicans built a large number of great religious centres, characterized by temples set upon high pyramidal platforms; these impressive edifices, together with the residential quarters of the priestly rulers, were set around rectangular courtyards, oriented so that the main temples would face the rising sun. The buildings were richly covered by sculpture and frescoes, and other lesser arts and crafts, such as pottery, weaving and the fashioning of beautiful objects in stone and jade, were well developed. Religion was evidently a major preoccupation, with an elaborate pantheon of elemental gods, and a calendar to regulate the religious festivities. The priesthood had developed a script (a form of picture-writing) and inscribed dates and astronomical calculations on specially erected stone stelae or on the walls of the buildings; it is clear that the priests had acquired a considerable knowledge of astronomy and mathematics. However, in their absorption with the mysteries of their exotic cults, they seem to have neglected more practical matters. Thus this otherwise highly developed civilization was somewhat lopsided. The principle of the wheel and the key-stone arch, to give two examples, were not discovered by people who could keep track of the phases of Venus.

Little is known of the social organization of the builders of these cities. Government was probably theocratic in character. The times seem to have been relatively peaceful; although warriors are depicted in the sculptures, it is the gods and the priests who get the limelight. Technical, artistic, cultural and religious ideas flowed freely from one city-state to another. But if there is a common pattern running through the Classic civilizations of Mexico (the influence of Teotihuacán was widespread) there were also wide regional differences in such matters as religious cults, styles of architecture, sculpture, pottery and so on, suggesting that the various city-states enjoyed a considerable measure of local autonomy.

Towards the end of the seventh century Teotihuacán appears to have been sacked and abandoned. Two centuries later the ceremonial centres in the Maya area were evacuated by their priestly rulers. The jungle closed in on them until only great scrub-covered mounds remained to excite the imagination of European explorers of a later age. To the later inhabitants of the Valley of Mexico the deserted and crumbling ruins of Teotihuacán became the subject of legend; it was thought to have been 'the Abode of the Gods'. During the centuries which followed, the whole of Mexico was in a state of turmoil. There were mass migrations of peoples. The great Valley of Mexico, with its rich cornfields and teeming villages and towns built around the lake, lay open and defenceless. It was a tempting target for the tough, semi-nomadic hunting tribes who wandered in the barren lands to the north. In the tenth century, one of these tribes, a Nahua-speaking people called the Toltecs, made themselves the masters of the Valley, establishing their capital at Tula[3] on its northern outskirts. From the sedentary valley folk, whom they conquered, the Toltecs acquired the basic arts and crafts of the Classic civilization, but this new civilization was a somewhat ruder version of what had gone before. The warrior was now as important in society as the priest. Religion was still all-important, but it was now bound up with war. The old Classic Rain God, Tlaloc, and Quetzalcoatl, the bringer of civilization, still occupied an important place in the pantheon, but they were now rivalled in importance by the bloodthirsty tribal gods of the hunting people. Human sacrifice, which seems to have been rare in Classic times, occupied a central position in the new cults. Great ceremonial centres were still built, but the cities of this new age tended to become more urban and secular in character. Fortifications make their appearance for the first time. From the relative peace and harmony of Classic times Mexico entered at this time into a period of religious dissension and war: what Professor Toynbee would call 'a time of troubles'.

THE AZTEC EMPIRE

After three centuries of precarious rule, Tula suffered the same fate as Teotihuacán, when a new wave of Chichimec invaders descended upon the valley and sacked the Toltec capital. But in the same way as the Toltecs had assumed the gods and way of life of Teotihuacán, so the new barbarians were quick to assimilate the rudiments of civilization, and settle down to become respectable citizens in the cities on the shore of the lake. The Aztecs were the last of these marauding tribes to enter the valley, arriving during the thirteenth century. They are pictured in the codices as wild skin-clad archers fighting the already settled Chichimec folk, the latter protected by stout jackets of quilted cotton and wielding formidable wooden swords, the blades of which were lined with obsidian. At first these newcomers led a wandering existence, living under the protection of the various Chichimec cities around the lakes and, as mercenaries, fighting their battles for them.

In 1325 the Aztecs halted at the south-western border of the principal lake, where, to borrow Prescott's words, 'they beheld perched on the stem of a prickly pear . . . a royal eagle of extraordinary size and beauty, with a serpent in his talons and his wings spread open to the rising sun'.[4] They hailed this as a sign of the gods, and founded their capital, Tenochtitlán, on the site of the miracle. The eagle and his serpent are now the national coat of arms of Mexico. In the years which followed, by a combination of diplomacy and war, the Aztecs extended their power, obtaining first the hegemony of the valley; later, in a series of military operations, they spread their influence from coast to coast, and even as far south as Chiapas and Guatemala. Tenochtitlán thus became the head of a predatory empire, subsisting on food and tribute paid by subject towns. But the Aztecs never managed to create a contented monolithic state such as that of the Inca of Peru. There were frequent wars and revolts.

Even in its greatest days Tenochtitlán was never more than the hated and bullying master of a large number of formerly independent and still dissident and resentful city-states.

Aztec society was still in a state of transition when the empire was brought to a sudden and premature end by the Spaniards in 1519. As wandering nomads, the Aztecs had maintained a simple tribal society, consisting of twenty clans, each of which regulated its own affairs. For more important decisions affecting the whole community the chosen leaders of the clans formed a tribal council, who appointed two chiefs. One chief – the most important in a time of trouble – led the tribe in war; the other looked after civil and religious affairs. In the course of three centuries this simple tribal society had to be adjusted to meet the needs of a great city-state and an empire. It underwent considerable changes, losing almost entirely the simple democratic spirit of the original tribal organization. Society became stratified; social classes emerged; and while the clans still handled local affairs, the central government became more autocratic.

At the time of the Conquest, the tribal council still in theory elected two chiefs, but the principal officer of state, the 'chief of men', was always chosen from the royal family. As a royal Head of State, Moctezuma stood above all other men, led his people in war, and was responsible for the external policy of the empire. The second great official of state, although always a man, was called 'the Snake Woman'. He conducted the internal affairs of the city, and was the custodian of religious and tribal custom. Beneath these two top executives there was a considerable bureaucracy. There were four basic social groups in Aztec society: the nobles, who filled most of the important posts in the imperial administration and were allowed to hold their own land; the commoners, who were members of a clan and worked land which could not be alienated – each family was allowed to possess and work its own plot in the communal land so long as it did not lie unused for over two years at a time; bondsmen, who tilled the estates of the nobles as serfs; and at the bottom of the social scale the porters and slaves, the latter being people who had either put themselves outside the pale of the law or had been captured in war. All those who tilled the land had to pay tribute, one-third of the product of the soil, in order to pay for the expenses of the state and maintain Moctezuma and his nobles in a suitable state of grandeur.

Occupying a favoured position in the hierarchy were the warriors.

The success of a warrior depended on the number of captives he brought home from his campaigns for the sacrificial altars, and the more successful he was the more elaborate the dress he was allowed to wear. The really outstanding warrior entered an order of knighthood, such as those of the eagle or the ocelot (tiger). He might also be given a grant of land in a conquered territory, or be provided with a larger than normal share of the tribute which flowed into Tenochtitlán from the conquered cities. In short, he entered the ranks of the nobility, which otherwise was the preserve of the members of the Royal House.

The priesthood, too, wielded enormous power in the community; for every important event of life – birth, education, war and death – was governed by religion. Only the priests could decide if the omens were good, whether it was merely a question of choosing a name for a child or deciding to wage war. The Aztecs acquired from their Toltec forerunners the complicated religious calendar and the pantheon of elemental gods of the Classic period. But the deity to whom they paid the greatest reverence was their own tribal god, Uitzilopochtli, a god of war, whose worship was closely related to that of the sun. His cult was based on the theory that this luminary derived its motive force from the blood-offerings of warriors captured in war. Should the supply of victims fail, the Aztecs thought, the processes of nature would stop. In accordance with this perverted philosophy, wars were conducted for the sole purpose of providing sacrificial victims, thousands of whom would be slain to celebrate a single victory. Moreover, these bloody practices spread to the cult of all the gods, and victims other than prisoners of war were sometimes sacrificed. We hear, for instance, of little children being led to Tlaloc's altar in the belief that, by sympathetic magic, their tears would induce a copious rainfall. Aztec religion was grim and horrible; one cannot whitewash it. But this *mania sanguinis* seems to have been an aberration of the warlike Chichimecs. It was not shared everywhere in ancient Mexico.

For example, if his mestizo descendant, the Texcocan chronicler, is to be believed, Netzahualcoatl, the philosopher king of the neighbouring city of Texcoco, held very different religious views, and actively discouraged the bloody practices of his time. He believed in an all-powerful and invisible deity, whom he called the 'Unknown God, the Cause of Causes', and in a heaven 'where all was eternal and corruption could not come'. 'The horrors of the tomb', he wrote in one of his poems, 'are but the cradle of the sun, and the dark shadows of death are brilliant lights for the stars.' He built a great temple of the usual pyramidal form, and upon the summit of it a tower of ten storeys, nine of which represented the nine heavens, the tenth being dedicated to this 'Invisible God'. The topmost storey of the tower was surmounted by a roof painted black, and profusely gilded with stars on the outside and encrusted with precious stones within. No image was allowed in the edifice, as unsuited to the Invisible God; and the people were expressly prohibited from profaning the altars with blood. Netzahualcoatl, according to his biographer, ruled his people with justice and loving-kindness, and delighted in the beautiful things of life – his flower-gardens and fountains, his aviaries of exotic birds – but his poetry was pessimistic, as well it might be, living as he did in an age of such brutality. 'All the earth is a grave and nothing escapes it', he wrote. 'Nothing is so perfect that it does not descend to the tomb.'

If the spiritual side of Aztec society was warped, its technical achievements were impressive, bearing in mind that Mexican civilization was still essentially in the Stone Age, such use of metals as was made – gold, silver, copper and bronze – being largely for ornamental purposes. The Aztecs were capable engineers, building great causeways and aqueducts and erecting huge pyramids and multi-roomed palaces. One may not like the sculpture, but can hardly fail to be impressed by its monumental size and brutal force. The Aztec warriors must have been a fine sight with their gorgeous raiment, feather headdresses, jewels and ornaments. Nor did the ordinary people lack the comforts of life, being equipped with every kind of household utensil, weapon and tool. Not that the Aztecs were great pioneers in the arts, nor was the spread of Aztec power a civilizing influence. Aztec culture, like that of all the contemporaneous Chichimec people, drew its inspiration from the Toltecs, and through the Toltecs from Teotihuacán. Some of the finest products which were on sale in the great market of Tlatelolco, such as the ceramics of Cholula and the beautiful gold-work of Azcapotzalco, were the handiwork of the direct descendants of Toltec craftsmen.

The Aztec economy depended upon agriculture, supplemented by tribute and trade. The ordinary free clansmen, working on their *chimalpas*, or floating gardens, were the backbone of the nation, economically. But as the Aztec conquests were extended, an ever-increasing quantity of tribute in kind – food, feather mantles, gold and jade – poured into Tenochtitlán. There was a special class of merchants, protected by their own god, who travelled far and wide through Middle America. The Aztecs exported from the valley obsidian, textiles, rope and other manufactured goods. They imported from the coastal regions shells, feathers, jade, and a wide range of tropical products. Trade was by barter; there was no money, but cacao beans were used in the markets for small change.

From this brief account of their history and achievements it should be clear that the Mexican Indians were people of character and ability, with considerable artistic taste and manual skill, a tendency towards mysticism in religion, a remarkable knowledge of astronomy and mathematics, but with only a Stone Age technology, apart from some ornamental metal work. Certain aspects of Aztec civilization are repugnant to modern susceptibilities, but it must be remembered that this warrior people had only recently emerged from barbarism; they lived in a world of malignant gods, who had to be propitiated, and were cursed by land hunger and perpetual warfare. The Aztec warrior elite was brought up from infancy, in Spartan fashion, to withstand cold and hunger and to be indifferent to pain, bloodshed and death. But it seems probable that the mass of the people in Aztec times, the farmers who tilled the fields or the serfs who laboured on the building of the mighty pyramids, were essentially the same long-suffering, tradition-bound folk that one meets today in a Mexican village – people who, while they may not always be at their best with foreigners, are good citizens in their own communities, polite, ceremonious, kind to children, and always ready to help a neighbour.

THE INDIAN LEGACY

How much of the Indian culture has survived? How important is this Indian heritage to modern Mexico? As we shall see, no sooner was Tenochtitlán destroyed by the Spaniards than the superstructure of the Aztec state was dismantled and replaced by the institutions of Spain. A white ruling class and bureaucracy displaced the Aztec nobles and warriors. All the Indians, whatever may have been their status in the past, were reduced to the rank of second-class citizens. Roman Catholic monks and friars took over from the gory Aztec priests; the sacred books of the Indians were burned; churches were built on the ruined foundations of the old temples. In short, the higher traits of the Indian culture disappeared. All that remained was an Indian peasantry whose way of life could not be changed so easily; indeed in the more remote parts of Mexico the type has persisted without fundamental change to the present day.

But the Indian peasants are fighting a losing battle against the advancing tide of 'mestization'. In 1810, after three centuries of interbreeding, some sixty per cent of the population was still reckoned to be purely Indian; the rest (except for a minute 0.3 per cent of purely white people) being classified as having mixed blood. Today the mingling of blood has gone so far that in the last census no attempt was made to classify the population on racial grounds; it provided social and economic data instead. Thus to a modern anthropologist a Mexican Indian is a man who persists in living like one, even though his blood may not any longer be pure. He is a peasant, living remote from a town in a small village or hamlet in the traditional way of his ancestors, growing maize, beans and squash on his small plot, probably still speaking his own native language, possessing picturesque handicrafts, wearing native dress, and rejoicing in a religion which, while superficially Christian, has retained a good many pagan features. Using such yardsticks, an American writer, Howard F. Cline,[5] has estimated that some thirty per cent of the population of modern Mexico still scrape a living as Indian peasants in what he calls 'remote Mexico'. This is probably as good an estimate as any of the size of the surviving Indian population.

Thus Mexico today is mainly a *mestizo* country. Except in the white upper crust of society most Mexicans have some Indian blood running in their veins; and with it, no doubt, there has been inherited omething of the Indian character. But heredity is something which cannot be measured. The culture, too, of modern Mexico is in part *mestizo*. Many Indian traits have survived in language, art, handicrafts, religion, folklore and even in such mundane matters as the cuisine. For example, some two and a half million Mexicans still speak a native language either as their only tongue or in addition to Spanish; and the Spanish spoken by all educated Mexicans incorporates many Indian words. Or consider the architecture of the colonial period. The successive architectural styles of the churches and monasteries – Gothic, Plateresque, Churrigueresque, etc. – are essentially European, but in the hands of Indian craftsmen they have been transformed into a unique Mexican blend, with a prodigality of ornament and a lavishness of decoration such as the Indian loves. A careful examination of the detail will reveal the use of pagan symbols, all mixed up with the saints, which somehow managed to get past the clerical censorship.

The village markets are still full of Indian handicrafts – pottery of every kind and shape, hand-woven *sarapes*, stamped leather belts, lacquered trays, etc. The techniques of manufacture are often very ancient. For example, in some of the villages Indian women can still be seen busily spinning with carved pottery spindle-whorls such as are commonly dug up by archeologists in the Aztec and Toltec strata. There has been no change at all since the Formative period in the make of the heavy stone mortars in which the maize is ground; the familiar 'clap clap' of the women as they slap the *tortillas* into shape must be one of the oldest sounds in Mexico. Many Indian dishes have survived and are enjoyed by modern Mexicans. For example, *mole* is a great delicacy: turkey covered by a thick and piquant sauce made from ground chiles, almonds, chocolate and spices, the recipe for which comes down straight from Aztec times.

It is not only in relation to the material arts and crafts that the Indian past intrudes into the present. The Spanish fathers, fortunately for the folklorists, were prepared to build upon pre-existing foundations of custom rather than destroy and build anew. Thus the Christianity of the modern Indian has a pagan basis. The Virgin miraculously made her appearance at precisely those places where there had flourished an ancient popular cult, so that the Indian pilgrims, as they flocked to the old shrines, hardly noticed that the object of their devotion had been changed.[6] It was at once the most practical and most merciful means of converting the Indians to the new Faith. Their pantheon had ever been elastic, incorporating the gods of both conquered and conquering tribes, and in the same way the Christian saints were easily absorbed. Though human sacrifice was now prohibited, some of the more harmless features of the old customs and beliefs remained. The rhythm of the old religious cycle was maintained, the seasonal festivals taking place at their accustomed times, with only minor adjustments needed to fit them in with the Christian calendar.

Every village and town in Mexico has its annual *fiesta*, usually in honour of a locally venerated Virgin or saint, but often with roots going back into the pagan past. Or sometimes the *fiesta* celebrates some historical event, such as the defeat of the Moors by the Spaniards, or the triumph of the Mexicans against the French in 1862. The Indian players and dancers dress up to fit their parts, wearing home-made knee breeches and capes to depict the Spanish *conquistador*, or donning the feathered head-dresses of Aztec warriors. The masks range from the fiercely mustachioed faces of caricatured white land-owners and officials, to those depicting birds and animals and devilish-looking gods. Sometimes the dress has incongruous modern touches, such as pink or purple stockings, or town boots encasing normally bare feet. The Mexican *fiesta* has its roots both in the Indian past and in the country villages of medieval Spain. Very often they are combined with market days, to which the Indians come from afar across the mountain trails with their goods loaded on the backs of mules and donkeys. The women sit at the stalls and do the trading, while the men get drunk and have a good time. Some of the *fiestas* are national in scope. For example, All Souls, in November, is cele-brated throughout Mexico as 'the Day of the Dead', a harvest festival marking the end of the annual cycle of growth. On this funereal occasion stalls all over Mexico display little skulls made of paper, candy or cake, and yellow flowers are placed on the graves – a take-over into Christianity of the pagan death motif. On a lighter note, at Christmas time, Mexican families celebrate *posadas* – gay parties during which sweets and fruits are hung aloft in a jar covered by paper and shaped like a pineapple – hence its name *piñata*. The game is for everybody to beat the piñata with a stick until it breaks, and a shower of sweets descends upon their heads.

Thus there are plenty of picturesque survivals in Mexico to remind one of the past; indeed it is these Indian touches which give Mexico its distinctive flavour, as compared with other countries of the Spanish world. Psychologically, the Indian influence in Mexico is felt in all sorts of subtle ways. But its importance should not be over-rated. The culture of the majority of educated Mexicans is basically Spanish; in the cities, it can perhaps be better described as a Spanish-Mexican version of an urban culture which is becoming more and more standardized in the industrial countries of the western world. What remains principally of the Indian culture is the anachronistic way of life of a hard-core minority of poor peasants, who have not yet been assimilated into modern life. However picturesque and 'typically Mexican' they may be, these survivors from the Indian past are a national liability from any progressive political point of view.

But while most Mexicans, for this reason, heartily dislike the tourists' view of their country as a land of quaint and picturesque survivals, the Indian past nevertheless occupies an important position in the national legend; indeed there is a tendency in some intellectual and political circles to inflate the Indians' part in the development of the nation, with a corresponding denigration of the role of Spain. It is understandable why this should be so. During the colonial period and the first hundred years of the republic, Mexico was ruled by a 'white' oligarchy of Spaniards and their locally-born descendants, with the Indians and the *mestizos* occupying an inferior position in society. The Mexican Revolution (see Chapter 7), which started in 1910, assumed very quickly the character of an Indian peasants' uprising against 'white' landlords. Later, as it developed an ideology, the Revolution was proclaimed to have as its objective the righting of wrongs suffered by the indigenous population following the Spanish Conquest and four centuries of white domination. The frescoes of Diego Rivera, Orozco and Siqueiros, which decorate many of the public buildings in Mexico, powerfully support this revolutionary propaganda theme, exalting the glories of Mexico's pre-Columbian past, and depicting the Revolution as the triumph of the oppressed Indians. In other words, the Indian has become identified in the public mind with the proletariat. For the *mestizo* intellectual of left-wing views, his Indian blood has the same inverted snob-appeal as a 'working-class background' for the student agitator in England or the USA. Thus Cuauhtémoc, the last of the Aztec Princes and the gallant defender of Tenochtitlán, has become for many Mexicans a symbol of the true spirit of Mexico. His statue looks down proudly on the busy traffic of the Paseo de la Reforma, but one searches in vain in the capital for a single statue commemorating the achievements of his formidable adversary and conqueror, Hernan Cortés.

4   The legacy of Spain

THERE MAY BE NO STATUE of Hernan Cortés in Mexico, but the shadow of this famous conqueror looms large over this once virgin Indian land. Wherever one looks in Mexico – in language, law, government, religion, culture, and in such physical manifestations as art and architecture – the imprint of Spain is unmistakable. It is only when it comes to assessing the value of this Spanish heritage that Mexican and foreign writers and historians differ, sometimes violently, in their opinions.

In the Protestant, English-speaking countries, and among Mexicans of liberal outlook, many people incline towards the so-called 'Black Legend' of Spain's record as a colonial power. In this one-sided version of history, which is usually combined with a romantic cult of the Indian, the Spaniards are given no credit at all for their achievement in conquering and civilizing the New World. They are depicted, without any redeeming features, as cruel and greedy conquerors who, in their insatiable lust for gold, subjected the Indian population to inhuman exploitation. Spanish colonial rule is portrayed as having produced nothing but a legacy of evil: a tradition of autocratic government, with no preparation made for any kind of democracy; a rigidly stratified and racially discriminatory society; an under-developed 'colonial' economy; huge agricultural estates, owned by a white oligarchy and worked by Indian peasants under conditions of feudal serfdom; and, providing the moral foundations of this exploitative white Establishment, a rich, subservient and reactionary Roman Catholic Church.

This jaundiced view of the Spanish record is vigorously opposed, however, by the upholders of the doctrine of *hispanidad*.[1] It is unfair, they point out, to apply twentieth-century standards of morality and politics to a sixteenth-century situation, and to blame the

Spaniards for everything which happened. Aztec society was no Garden of Eden, and indeed was inferior in most ways to the civilization of Renaissance Europe which the Spaniards brought with them to the New World. Above all, the Conquest was instrumental in bringing the light of Christianity to a pagan and barbarous people, freeing the Indians from the tyranny of their gory priests, and eliminating human sacrifice and cannibalism from their society. Rather than exterminating the Indians, as the English colonists did in North America, the Spaniards put them to work. In return for their labours and tribute (and the mass of the people had both laboured and paid tribute under their Aztec rulers) the Indians received, not only the blessings of Christianity, but all sorts of material advantages as well, such as new crops, draught animals, ploughs and the use of iron tools. Politically, too, they were better off; by contrast with the anarchy and constant warfare of the Aztec state, Mexico enjoyed under Spanish rule three hundred years of peace; for the first time in its history the country was unified, and provided with a common language, law, religion and government.

Both these exaggerated versions of Mexican colonial history are based on carefully selected facets of the truth. The real truth, no doubt, lies hidden somewhere in the grey area which, in human affairs, almost always separates white from black. Certainly, Cortés and his rough companions were no choir of angels; but neither for that matter were the Aztec warriors who indulged in war for its own sake, or the blood-spattered Indian priests who had no compunction about cutting out the hearts of thousands of victims in order to celebrate a single victory. The Spanish Conquest of Mexico is one of those epic stories, in the telling of which the common virtues and vices of the human race have been magnified beyond their normal dimensions. On both sides of this homeric struggle the contenders showed remarkable valour and determination; but there were also many acts of cruelty and treachery. An important motive of the conquerors was no doubt a thirst for gold and booty; indeed a financial dividend was necessary to pay the expenses of the expedition and obtain the interest and support of the Spanish Crown. But, mixed up with the greed, and perhaps more important as a motivating force, was a combination of missionary zeal – a crusading desire to convert the infidel for the glory of God – and a quixotic love of adventure for its own sake.

The story of the Conquest of Mexico has often been told – and never better than by that old soldier, Bernal Díaz, who took part in the expedition.[2] The barest recital of the facts must suffice here. On Good Friday of 1519, Hernan Cortés disembarked a pitifully small army of 555 men and 16 horses on the sand dunes of the Mexican coast, close to the modern port of Vera Cruz. Having burnt his boats, so as to make it impossible for the waverers in his army to think of retreat, he boldly led this tiny force inland into the unknown. It was a formidable march; first through the tropical scrub of the coastal strip; then up the steep escarpment of the Eastern Sierra Madre, some ten thousand feet of hard climbing; at length the tired soldiers in their heavy armour emerged from the wilderness of high mountains on to the broad plain of the central plateau, the heartland of the Aztec Empire. Observing with jubilation and awe the rich fields of maize in the valleys, the teeming cities with their magnificent palaces and gruesome temples, and greeted in each town by gorgeously attired emissaries bearing gifts of gold and jade, it must have seemed to the simple Spanish soldiers that here was El Dorado at last, the real thing and not merely a mirage. As for the Indians, they were at first too bemused by the strange appearance of these white-faced visitors from another world, with their unbelievable horses and terrifying guns, to think of putting up any serious resistance.

The first real battle which Cortés had to fight was against the warlike Tlaxcalans, who stood athwart his path, having nerved themselves to take up arms against the intruders. But the superior technology of the Spaniards prevailed over native valour. The victorious Cortés, who was as adept in diplomacy as in soldiering, being informed that the Tlaxcalans were hereditary enemies of the Aztecs and had never been subdued, then proceeded to win over this tough warrior people to his side. With his army thus reinforced (some of the coastal Indian tribes, who had been conquered by the Aztecs, were already supporting his cause), the campaign began almost to assume the guise of a war of liberation, as the combined Spanish and Indian forces marched towards the Aztec capital.

Moctezuma, waiting anxiously in his island fortress of Tenochtitlán, was overcome by indecision and superstitious awe as the pale-faced strangers and their Indian allies took up station on the edge of the great lake. According to Aztec legend, the fair god,

Quetzalcoatl, the culture-hero of the Toltecs, had promised that one day he would return from the land of the rising sun to which he had retired. Was this a divine visitation? To fight or not to fight? At length, having consulted the omens, this Hamlet-like Prince decided to receive the Spaniards in his capital as honoured guests. It was a fatal decision. In repayment of the Emperor's hospitality, Cortés, in a daring coup, made Moctezuma a prisoner in his own capital, and, by this single blow struck at the centre of power, became the temporary master of the Valley of Mexico. With their emperor held as a hostage, the Aztec warriors were at first too stunned and overawed to attempt retaliation.

But nine months later, when Cortés was compelled to return to the coast to deal with a force of Spaniards who had been sent to arrest him (he was at odds with his official chief in Cuba), the Aztec warriors, provoked beyond endurance, rose up in their wrath, and after a fearful struggle the Spanish garrison was driven from the Aztec capital with heavy losses. Cortés, who had rushed back to the rescue (having defeated and won over to his cause the intruding Spaniards on the coast) is said to have sat down under a tree and wept on this night (La Noche Triste) of bitter defeat.[3] But he was not the man to repine. In 1521, having reinforced the Indian contingent of his army and built landing craft, he crossed the lake and mounted a concerted attack upon the Aztec capital. Advancing slowly and steadily into the city, the Spaniards systematically wrecked everything which stood in their path, until the once glorious Tenochtitlán was in ruins, its streets and canals littered with rubble and the putrefying corpses of the dead. Although defeated, the heroic last-ditch defence of their capital was the Aztecs' finest hour. Cuauhtémoc, the new emperor, refused to surrender on any terms until he was captured and forced at gun-point to submit. Even under torture he maintained a stoical calm. But Indian valour was of no avail. Cortés was now truly the master of Mexico, although it would not be until 1545, after some further arduous campaigns, that the whole of the future colony of New Spain had been pacified.

THE COLONIAL GOVERNMENT

In far distant Spain the news of this great achievement was received with enthusiasm. Cortés was the hero of the hour, his earlier sins temporarily forgotten. On 15 October 1522 the Emperor Charles V appointed him as Governor, Captain General and Chief Justice of the new colony. But no sooner had the ink dried on the parchment of this commission than the young monarch, under the influence of jealous courtiers, began to have second thoughts about the wisdom of entrusting so much power to the great *conquistador*. Two Spanish notaries were hastily dispatched to Mexico, ostensibly to verify that the King's royal fifth of the booty was being exacted, but in fact to spy on Cortés.

Thus in the very first year after the Conquest there began to open the rift which, throughout the three hundred years of the Spanish colony, was to divide the Spanish settlers in the New World from the royal government in Spain. At first the controversy centred upon the institution known as *encomienda*, by means of which it was customary at this time for the leaders of successful Spanish expeditions to reward themselves and the most deserving of their followers. Through a formal grant, designated Indian families, usually the inhabitants of a town or clusters of towns, were entrusted to the charge of a Spanish colonist. The latter, known as the *encomendero*, was permitted to exact tribute from his Indians in the form of commodities and labour service. In return he was expected to render military service to the colony and provide for the christianization of the Indians committed to his charge. In short the *encomendero* was essentially a feudal lord, but one whose wealth was derived from the control of manpower and its product rather than from the ownership of real property. The Indian villages retained their communal lands. The great landed estate, or *hacienda*, was something which developed at a later stage in the history of the colony.

Humanitarian protests of Dominican priests about the abuses of the system led to the laws of Burgos (1512–13), which sanctioned *encomienda*, but sought, by regulation, to protect the Indians from unjust exploitation by the Spanish settlers. In 1520, the year before the fall of Tenochtitlán, the royal government, under pressure from the Dominican friar Bartolomé de las Casas, an ardent champion of the Indian cause, ruled that the entire system of *encomienda* should come to an end. But this was not practical politics in Mexico. Cortés, in 1521, had to be given the means of satisfying both his own ambitions and those of his followers. Indian labour was essential to enable them to exploit the conquered territories and, indeed, for the survival of the colony – for it was not in the tradition of the Spanish knight to soil his hands with menial toil. And so, under a shower of petitions from the colonists, the Emperor was forced reluctantly to give way. Cortés, with the title of a Marquis, became the greatest *encomendero* of them all, with vast holdings in the Valley of Oaxaca. His followers, in accordance with their deserts, were likewise suitably rewarded.

This concession to the settlers by the Crown was no more than a tactical withdrawal. Cortés was relieved of his governorship in 1526, and the advance guard of the Spanish bureaucracy moved in. In 1535, the first viceroy of Mexico, Antonio de Mendoza, arrived from Spain. A tendency of the *encomiendas* to become hereditary in the leading colonial families was rudely halted by the 'New Laws' of 1542–43, which, among many other restrictions, set a limit to the time for which these grants could be held. The new measures caused a rebellion of the settlers in Peru; but in Mexico a cautious viceroy, gauging the strength of local feeling on this issue, refrained from announcing them. Even so, much restrictive legislation remained in effect, and as the generations succeeded one another, the institution of *encomienda* gradually died. Government-appointed District Commissioners, known as *corregidores*, progressively took over the administration of native affairs and the collection of tribute. The members of the local 'Creole' aristocracy (Mexican-born white settlers), deprived of their *encomiendas*, and indeed without being allowed to play any significant part in the government of the colony – it was run almost entirely by peninsular Spaniards – were forced to seek new outlets for their ambitions and new sources of wealth in the ownership of mines, cattle ranches and vast agricultural estates. They remained wealthy but were deprived of all political power.

All authority in the colony stemmed from the Spanish crown; there was no local autonomy of any kind. The viceroy, as the representative of the monarch, was surrounded by all the trappings of royalty. He was the supreme executive authority in military and administrative matters; but the powers of even this august official, who was invariably appointed from Spain for a term of years, was limited by checks and balances. From the Royal Council of the Indies in Spain, the fount of colonial policy, there issued a stream of laws and instructions, covering every aspect of government in the most meticulous detail. Locally, the viceroy was 'assisted' – counter-balanced might be a better word – by the *audiencia*, a judicial body, responsible directly to the Council in Spain and staffed by eminent Spanish jurists, which served as the ultimate appellate tribunal in the colony. It had the power to hear appeals against the viceroy or make complaints against his administration. It also exercised a general supervision over the conduct of inferior magistrates, and had an over-all responsibility for Indian affairs. Viceroy, *audiencia*, provincial governors, *corregidores* and the learned clerks (*escribanos*), who provided the nucleus of a civil service – these together constituted the machinery of colonial government. There were no popular or parliamentary institutions of any kind above the level of municipal councils (*cabildos*); and these bodies were only democratic in theory. Municipal offices, such as *alcalde* and *regidor*, were monopolized by the local oligarchy and became virtually hereditary in certain families.

On the other hand, although autocratic, the colonial government was paternalistic in its attitude towards its Indian subjects. Although there was a mass of legislation designed to regulate such matters as the conditions under which tribute could be collected, or the recruitment of Indians under the system of *repartimiento* for forced labour in the mines and on public works, the law was not strong enough to reach very far into the countryside. The viceroys were usually men of high calibre drawn from the Spanish nobility or the higher ranks of the Church. But in the lower levels of the bureaucracy, as was customary in Europe at this time, offices were bought and sold, being regarded as investments because of their perquisites, rather than as positions of trust.

These mercenary officials waxed rich from a number of lucrative rackets. For example, the collection of tribute was farmed out to the Indian chiefs in the villages, who acted as middlemen between their own people and the Spanish *corregidores*. These petty officials were only interested in lining their own pockets at the expense of their unfortunate charges, from whom was squeezed every drop of tribute that could be collected. Again, the *corregidores* managed to obtain the monopoly for selling European goods to the Indians, on the argument that ignorant peasants would be cheated by private traders. Instead they were cheated by the *corregidores*. Using their position of power, these officials forced the impecunious peasants to buy goods they could not afford, and indeed did not even want. Loaded with debts, which they could only pay off by work, the Indians were virtually enslaved by this means, although in theory they remained free men under the law. But of all the exactions to which the Indians were subjected by far the most onerous and disruptive was the system of *repartimiento*, under which, in defiance of the regulations, whole villages were denuded of their male inhabitants, who were forced to leave their homes in order to work, under the cruellest possible conditions, in the silver mines. Thus the benevolent intentions of the royal government in far-distant Spain towards the Indians were very largely thwarted, and it was mainly the white population which benefited from Spanish rule.

THE CHURCH IN COLONIAL TIMES

In the early colonial period, the best friends and protectors of the Indians were the Roman Catholic friars, who set about their immense task of converting the natives to the true Faith with the utmost fervour and devotion, and did their best, but not always with success, to protect their charges from the exactions of the settlers. The Spanish Church at this time had been undergoing a process of reform and purification, and was inspired by the spirit of humanism. The friars went barefoot and unarmed in deliberate contrast to the mounted and gaily bedecked Spanish cavaliers. They saw their mission as being not merely to convert the Indians to Christianity, but also to bring them the benefits of European civilization. Thus the first Bishop of Mexico, Juan de Zumárraga, who was appointed in 1527, lent his support – he was a disciple of Erasmus – to the foundation of a College of Tlatelolco in which Indians of the upper class were taught Latin, rhetoric, logic, music and philosophy; a colleague, Vasco de Quiroga, established model communities of Indian villagers patterned on Thomas More's Utopia; the Franciscan friar, Bernardino de Sahagún, an anthropologist before his time, wrote in the Nahuatl language, of which he became a master, an encyclopedic work on the civilization of the Aztecs.

Once the initial task of converting the Indians had been completed, the missionary zeal began to fade, except in isolated pockets on the still untamed frontiers. Among the sedentary Indians of the plateau, it was not long before Christian churches had replaced the pagan temples, and the people had settled down to an ostensibly Christian way of life. As this happened, secular clergy, working under the discipline of episcopal authority, were appointed to replace the friars. The great crusade was over, and religious work in the villages settled down into an uninspired routine. Meanwhile the Church in Mexico became both powerful and rich. By Papal Bulls of 1501 and 1508, the Spanish Crown had obtained the power (*Patronato Real*) to appoint churchmen in the colonies, to administer ecclesiastical jurisdictions, and even to veto Papal Bulls. By these means the Church in Mexico became almost like a branch of the colonial government, and ecclesiastics were appointed to many high political posts. As for wealth, the Church became the biggest landowner in Mexico; ostentatious living replaced the self-sacrificing austerity of the early days.

THE COLONIAL ECONOMY

Agriculture was the most important economic activity of the colony, its output surpassing in market value the product of the mines. The principal crop was maize, the staple food of the Indians. Only enough wheat was grown for consumption by the white colonists; considerable quantities of sugar and other tropical products were exported. Because of the restrictive policies of the Spanish government many potentially valuable crops, such as chocolate, vanilla, cochineal and cotton, which had flourished in Aztec times, were neglected. The methods of agriculture continued to be primitive, for the Indians did not take willingly to the new crops or such innovations as the European plough. Meanwhile the manpower available for agriculture suffered a disastrous decline as the result of epidemics of European diseases such as measles and smallpox. According to one estimate the Indian population of New Spain declined from about 25 million in 1519 to slightly over one million in 1605, a truly appalling rate of depopulation.[4]

The consequences for Mexican agriculture were disastrous. With a drastic reduction in the number of Indian peasants and a decline in agricultural output, the *encomiendas* ceased to be profitable. Previously fertile agricultural areas were abandoned, and either given over to sheep-raising (ranching became a major industry) or allowed to run wild. The Spanish settlers, in search of a new source of revenue, began buying tracts of land, some of which had previously been the communal property of the villages, to form farming estates (*haciendas*), many of them of huge size. To attract labour, and keep it, the system of peonage was developed, under which the Indians were given small plots of land in the *hacienda* for their own use, in return for work and services of different kinds to the landlord. To make doubly sure of their servitude the Indians were compelled to buy their meagre requirements from the *hacienda* store, in this way running up debts which could only be paid off by work. Thus as the *encomiendas* disappeared, the *haciendas* took over as the main source of wealth, power and prestige for the white ruling class, and so they remained until the Revolution of 1910 put an end to this system of exploitation. Only in the more remote areas of Mexico, and mostly on poor land, did the Indians continue to cultivate the traditional *ejidos* in their own self-contained communities.[5]

Mining occupied the second place in the colonial economy. In the mother country gold and silver were prized as the principal rewards of empire, without anybody realizing the inflationary consequences of their importation on such a large scale. Shortly after the conquest, as explorers moved into the waste-lands of northern Mexico, rich deposits of silver were discovered in such places as Guanajuato, Zacatecas and San Luis Potosí, and flourishing colonial towns, entirely Spanish in their architecture and layout, came into being in these mining regions. Silver was also mined at Real de Monte near Pachuca, and in Taxco in the south. Silver became one of Mexico's principal items of export, but the production of base metals, such as copper, lead and zinc, of which Mexico has rich supplies, was almost entirely neglected at this time.

Trade between Mexico and the outside world was rigidly controlled on the then prevailing mercantile principle that the function of a colony was to produce raw materials, and especially precious metals, for the benefit of the mother country, taking in return the manufactured products of Spain. The handling of this two-way trade was monopolized by a guild of Spanish merchants in Seville, the *Consulado*, and its opposite numbers in the colonies, the *Consulados* of Mexico City and Lima in Peru. Such a closed system of trade was productive of high prices, inefficiency and graft, and inevitably led to a good deal of smuggling and other forms of black marketing. The development of national industry was discouraged by the Spanish authorities. The principal local products were cigars and cigarettes, manufactured as a monopoly in the royal tobacco factories; hides, tallow and leather goods as a by-product of the cattle ranches (the countryside teemed with horses, mules, cattle, sheep and goats); and textiles, produced by private enterprise, under the most appalling conditions of hardship and squalor, in small sweat-shops known as *obrajes*.

COLONIAL SOCIETY

By the end of the colonial period the decline in the population had been arrested; indeed the numbers had begun to increase once more, having reached a level of some six million. Society was divided into three main classes, each with their own sub-divisions: at the top, a white ruling minority of some 15,000 people, comprising the penin-sular Spaniards (*Gachupines*)[6] and the more numerous locally-born white settlers (*Creoles*); at the bottom of the social structure, more than three and a half million Indians; between these two pure racial groups, an increasing population of people of mixed blood, mainly *mestizo* (i.e. of Indian and Spanish blood), but in some cases, especially in the coastal regions, with a negro admixture resulting from the importation of African slaves.

As in Spain at this time (and as they had been in Mexico in Aztec times), class distinctions were rigid, but with the added complication in colonial society of racial as well as economic and social differences. At the summit of the hierarchy the Spanish-born *Gachupines* occupied all the best posts in the colonial administration. From this eminence they looked down upon the white Creole settlers with much the same disdain as that of a member of the British raj for the Anglo-Indian. The Creoles strongly resented this haughty attitude; not that we can feel too sorry for them. Many of them were extremely rich men, the owners of *haciendas*, mines and houses, who disliked the peninsular Spaniards but aped their manners and dress, being more Spanish than the Spaniards in their attitude towards life and their romantic attachment to the Spanish Crown. Deprived of responsi-bility, the Creoles tended to be somewhat frivolous, spending much of their time gossiping with friends, ogling the ladies during the evening *paseo*, showing off the paces of their horses in the full glory of *charro* costume, and attending bull-fights and masses. For the white upper class in Mexico, both Spanish and Creole, life was gracious and elegant. Society centred upon the glittering viceregal court. The ladies, clad in expensive silks from China, were loaded with jewels. There were balls, theatres and concerts; art and literature (the latter of a somewhat recondite kind) flourished. In short, Mexico

City at this time was the most polished and indeed probably the most civilized city of the western hemisphere.

At the base of the social pyramid the Indians lived at a bare level of subsistence either as peons on the *haciendas*, or on their *ejidos* in the more remote parts of the country. Except in some of the untamed tribes on the frontiers, the warlike spirit of the Aztecs had long since disappeared – the Indians were humble and obsequious in the presence of white men, their real feelings hidden behind a mask of apathy. There was no longer any Indian upper class in Mexico apart from some rich village *caciques* who had made money by acting as middlemen for the *corregidores*. The attempt of the Church in the sixteenth century to educate the Indian elite into the ways of European civilization had long since been abandoned. Thus the old Indian hierarchy of nobles, warriors, priests, peasants and slaves had disappeared. Only the peasants remained, tilling their small plots of land as they had done since time immemorial.

The *mestizos*, although destined to become the backbone of the Mexican republic, occupied in colonial times an uncomfortable middle position between the white upper class and the Indians, being excluded from the privileges of the conquering race, but lacking the protection of the laws which treated the Indians as wards of the Crown. The mestizos had to make do, as best they could, as ranchers, miners, artisans, shopkeepers and in other such middle-class occupations. Many fell by the wayside and joined the ranks of the 20,000 beggars, or *leperos*, in the capital – poor, often hideously diseased, creatures, who begged for alms during the day and terrorized the city during the night. Others joined the bands of brigands who infested the highways of colonial Mexico. Unlike the apathetic Indians and the soft, luxury-loving Creoles, the *mestizos* combined in their character something of the stoic qualities of the Indian and the volcanic and explosive energy of the Spanish *conquistadores*. They were the perfect fodder for a revolution; but their time had not yet come. First the Creoles had to have their turn.

Some knowledge of the colonial period is essential for an understanding of modern Mexico; for, as will be seen, most of the problems (for example the stratification of society and a tradition of authoritarian government) with which the republic has had to grapple had their roots in the colonial past. Indeed Mexican history makes little sense if it is interpreted in terms of British or North American experience or morality. For instance, in the English colonies of North America, democracy found its roots in the town meeting and the representative assembly; there were no similar bodies to foster the democratic impulse in Spanish America. Or again, in the New England colonies, there was at first no racial problem, because the wild Indian tribes of the East coast were exterminated. In Mexico, in contrast, a deep-rooted Indian peasantry was in occupation of the land, providing a ready-made proletariat. Thus, unlike the egalitarian and freedom-loving Pilgrim fathers, who had to work with their own hands, the Spanish settlers from the beginning regarded themselves as gentlemen; their outlook was that of the Spanish *hidalgo*, being more concerned with honour and dignity than with the individual rights associated with the Anglo-Saxon tradition. No doubt, each of these two divergent streams of American civilization has its particular virtues and vices. Rather than compare one with the other, it is safer merely to recognize that they are different.

5   The young republic

ON SUNDAY MORNING, 16 September 1810, Father Miguel Hidalgo y Costillo, parish priest of the small town of Dolores in central Mexico, tolled the bells of his church to summon his flock. Climbing into his pulpit, he delivered to his small-town congregation what has come to be regarded as Mexico's declaration of independence. With shouts of 'Viva México, long live the Virgin of Guadalupe, and death to the Spaniards!' Indians and *mestizos* all over the country responded to the call of this fiery priest, arming themselves with knives, clubs, machetes and any other weapons that came to hand. The orgy of killing and pillage which followed shook the Spanish colony to its foundations.

The sudden explosion of popular fury, sparked by Hidalgo's oratory, was the cumulative result of three hundred years of oppression, suffered in silence and with patience until in the eighteenth century the ideas of the Enlightenment, with their stress upon freedom and equality, rationalism and the rights of man, began to seep into the colony. The philosophy of Descartes and Locke now competed with scholasticism in the University of Mexico, and even some of the priests were infected by the new doctrines. There was also a new look in politics. In 1700 a French Bourbon monarch took over in Spain from the decadent Hapsburg dynasty. The third King of this line, Charles III (1759–88), imbued with French conceptions of administrative efficiency, despatched an emissary, José de Gálvez, to Mexico to look over the cumbersome structure of colonial administration; and some sweeping changes were made on his recommendation. Mexico got one of her best Viceroys in Antonio de Bucareli (1771–79); twelve Spanish-appointed intendants replaced the corrupt and greedy provincial *corregidores*; and the treatment of the Indians was greatly improved in such matters as the collection of tribute and the administration of forced labour. In line with the new trend towards laissez-faire in economics, the old, unpopular restrictions on Mexican trade were partially lifted; Mexico was now permitted to trade with all the Spanish ports, and the tariffs were lowered. But these popular, if belated reforms, far from removing the grievances of the colonists, only served to whet their appetite for more. Beneath the surface of a Mexico which had remained feudal and Catholic under the autocratic rule of the Spanish Kings and their officials, there began to stir the desire, at first not for complete independence from Spain, but for a much greater measure of local autonomy.

These yearnings for more freedom were intensified by a series of dramatic events in the outside world – the successful revolt of the British North American colonies; the French Revolution; and most devastating of all in its impact upon colonial loyalties, Napoleon's occupation of Spain in 1808, and the placing of his brother Joseph on the proud throne of Castile. The Creoles in Mexico responded to this event by declaring their undying loyalty to the deposed and imprisoned Spanish King, Ferdinand VII, and demanding of the viceroy that, in default of a properly constituted Spanish government, they should be allowed to establish their own Junta in Mexico to run the colony. But the peninsular Spaniards in Mexico, seeing through this Creole trick, insisted that the Mexican colony must take its orders from the pro-Ferdinand Juntas which had been set up in various parts of Spain to carry on the struggle against Napoleon. When the weak and venal Viceroy, José de Iturrigary, showed signs of favouring the Creoles, the local Spaniards took the law into their own hands, and, in a swift *coup d'état*, replaced him with a nominee of their own choosing. The discomforted Creoles, cheated of their prize, began actively to conspire against this arbitrarily imposed colonial government, forming themselves into small secret groups throughout the country.

Hidalgo became a member of one such conspiratorial group in Querétaro, which was headed by a local Creole army officer and landowner, Ignacio Allende. The latter, a typical member of his class, had no ambition beyond freeing his country from the hated Spanish officials and replacing them, under the authority of King Ferdinand, by local officers and gentlemen of his own kind. But the priest, Hidalgo, was a man of a different stamp – an idealist well versed in the revolutionary literature of France, and with a strong sympathy for the oppressed Indians. Impetuous by nature, and learning that Allende's plot for a military revolt had been discovered by the Spanish authorities, he decided to launch his own appeal for an uprising, relying upon the support of the people. The response to his call was immediate and overwhelming. Almost overnight the former parish priest, to the vast annoyance of Allende, found himself in the position of general, being led by, rather than leading, an uncontrollable rabble of armed citizens, who proceeded with ferocious valour to give battle to the regular forces of the Spanish army. Town after town in central and northern Mexico was seized by the revolutionaries, who ransacked the houses and properties of both the Spaniards and the wealthy Creoles, and massacred every white man, woman and child upon whom they could lay their hands. Soon there were guerrilla bands at large all over the country, raiding the *haciendas*, and looting the silver trains and caravans of the Spanish merchants. Although Hidalgo had not intended anything so drastic, this was a real bloody revolution, a veritable war of the castes. Every white man in the colony, whether Spaniard or locally born, trembled for his life.

With his makeshift army grown to 80,000 men, Hidalgo marched on the capital, and almost certainly could have taken it. But at the last moment he turned back. Being a humane man, he may have feared the carnage which would have resulted had he set his mob loose on the defenceless city. This decision to retreat was the turning point in his fortunes. Gradually the tough Spanish General, Félix Calleja, with his more disciplined troops, gained the upper hand, and a terrible vengeance was wreaked upon the revolutionaries in every town which was recaptured. As so often happens in civil wars, especially one with racial undertones, both sides were guilty of the most frightful atrocities.

In 1811 Hidalgo was captured and executed. A *mestizo* parish priest, José María Morelos, a friend and disciple of Hidalgo, assumed the leadership of the revolution, with command of a small guerrilla force in the rugged mountains of Guerrero. Morelos was not only a better soldier than Hidalgo, but more astute as a politician. His revolutionary aims were codified by a Congress over which he presided in Chilpancingo, in 1813. Democratic government, racial equality, the abolition of clerical and military privileges, the restoration of land to the dispossessed Indians – his programme anticipated by a hundred years what would be some of the main planks of the Mexican Revolution. But he was too far in advance of his time. Morelos was captured and executed in 1815. By 1819 the Spanish authorities were once again in almost full control of the colony; only two of the revolutionary leaders, both destined to be Presidents of Mexico, were still at large; Guadalupe Victoria, in hiding in the jungles of Vera Cruz, and Vicente Guerrero, of Indian peasant origin, who held out with a small guerrilla force in the mountains of the State which today bears his name.

Independence, when it finally came to Mexico, was something of an anticlimax. In 1820 the liberals in Spain obtained control of the Spanish government and forced King Ferdinand VII (who had been restored to his throne in 1815) to accept a democratic constitution. This liberal victory was not at all to the taste of the reactionary bishops and landowners in Mexico, who had had their fill of 'democracy' during the revolution of Hidalgo and Morelos. Rather an independent Mexico than a colonial government dominated by the liberals in Spain, argued the Mexican conservatives, who had fought against the revolution; and they found a willing tool for this policy in a young, debonair, and unscrupulous Creole soldier, Agustín de Iturbide. Ordered by the Viceroy to hunt down the elusive Vicente Guerrero, Iturbide succeeded instead in coming to terms with this guerrilla leader. Under the Plan of Iguala, it was agreed by the two men that Mexico should become an independent monarchy. This proposal suited the conservatives admirably; and with immediate independence as the bait, the liberals in Mexico were also induced to support the plan, even though it meant a postponement of their own more radical plans for the institution of democracy and social reform. Thus, in 1821, when a new Viceroy, Juan O'Donojú, landed in Vera Cruz as the representative of the liberal government in Spain, he found Iturbide, at the head of a large army, blocking his path. Before reaching the capital, he was induced to sign a document (subsequently repudiated by Ferdinand VII) conceding the formal independence of Mexico, but on the understanding that a Spanish Prince would be invited to occupy the throne of the new country.

On 27 September 1821, Iturbide rode into Mexico City in triumph at the head of his army, and was received by the population with jubilation. In the following year – since Spain had refused to recognize the independence of Mexico – Iturbide persuaded the Mexican Congress to crown him as Emperor. Agustín I, Emperor of Mexico! The Creole adventurer had achieved more than his wildest dreams, and he spent some wonderful months, turning members of his family into princes and princesses, and designing gorgeous uniforms and decorations for his courtiers and generals. But his dream-empire was built upon a volcano. He soon lost the support of the revolutionary leaders, Guadalupe Victoria and Guerrero, and the Mexican liberals. Faced by bankruptcy and mounting chaos, he tried to rule as an autocrat and disbanded the Congress. Thereupon some of the generals, including Victoria and Guerrero, revolted, with the demand that Congress should be restored. A disillusioned Iturbide abdicated in May 1823, and went abroad.[1] The restored Congress, now dominated by the local liberals, produced a new constitution, taking that of the USA as their model. Thus Mexico, in 1824, became, in theory at least, a democratic federal republic. Guadalupe Victoria, a hero of the revolution, was elected to become the new republic's first President.

GROWING PAINS

It is one thing for a group of enthusiastic, but totally inexperienced, amateur politicians to draft a democratic constitution on paper; quite another thing to make it work in a country with no tradition of, nor any preparation for democracy. For the immediate result of independence had been, not a social revolution such as Hidalgo and Morelos had hoped for, but merely a transfer of power from the peninsular Spaniards to the local Creole aristocracy. Society was still as sharply divided on racial, social and economic lines as it had been during the time of the colony.

Democracy could not be expected to function, let alone flourish, in a country in which the majority of the inhabitants were illiterate Indian peasants. The electoral basis was too narrow, being confined to the upper crust of Creoles and the still quite small *mestizo* middle class. The vested interests of the landowners, army and the Roman Catholic Church – and increasingly too of foreign capitalists – were immensely strong. A President who ignored or threatened these powerful pressure groups did so at his peril.

Thus money and military power counted for more than votes. Patronage, rather than ideology, was the motive force in politics.

A President could only retain the support of his followers, and perhaps buy off some of his enemies, by rewarding them with jobs in the bureaucracy or in the army. But it was not easy to find the money to support the generals and officials in suitable opulence and splendour. The country was bankrupt. The wars of independence had caused a great deal of destruction. Many of the mines were closed, and the *haciendas* had been denuded of their manpower by recruitment of the Indians into rival armies. There was no effective system of taxation, and nobody available in the republic with any experience of fiscal management. Thus successive governments had resorted to printing paper money, or borrowing funds from abroad on exorbitant terms. Failing these expedients, the only remedy was to raid the well-endowed and immensely rich Roman Catholic Church – by far the greatest landowner in Mexico. But to attack the Church was asking for trouble; for there was always a general waiting on the side-lines, ready to leap to the defence of Mother Church in the sacred name of religion.

Military *coups d'état* happened with dreary regularity, interspersed with an occasional rigged election. Sporadic attempts at democratic rule, whether under a federal or centralistic form of government, invariably degenerated into anarchy, and were followed by periods of dictatorship. Politics was like a game of musical chairs. During the first fifty years of the republic over thirty individuals served as president, leading more than fifty governments.[2] A president was lucky if he stayed in power for two years; sometimes he survived for only a few months. On a number of occasions two men simultaneously claimed to be the legitimate president, with rival governments exercising their authority in different parts of the country.

There were two main groups in politics: the conservatives and the liberals. The conservatives represented essentially the vested interests of the Creole landowners, the Church and the army. Having achieved independence from Spain, they were content that society should remain much the same as it had been in colonial times, with the Indians and the *mestizos* kept firmly in their places, socially and economically, and working for the benefit of the white upper class. Being realists, they had no illusions about democracy. They were prepared to support any political leader – almost always a soldier – who was willing and able to play their game and provide the necessary degree of strong government.

The Mexican liberals, in contrast, as the spiritual heirs of Hidalgo and Morelos, stood on a platform of democracy and social reform. They realized that democracy could never flourish in Mexico until the power of the triple-tiered conservative establishment had been broken. In particular, the Church must be made to disgorge its wealth, education freed from clerical control, and the clergy deprived of its privileges and immunities (*fueros*). The same applied to the army, which likewise had its own military courts and, protected by its *fueros*, lived a life of its own outside the law. On social reform, the liberals were divided between the *Moderados*, who were strong believers in the virtues of private property and laissez-faire in economics, and were more interested in implanting Anglo-Saxon institutions of democracy than in obtaining social justice for the under-privileged; and the more radical *Puros* who demanded not only the abolition of clerical and military *fueros* and the confiscation of clerical property, but also the destruction of caste distinctions. Disciples of Rousseau, Jefferson, and Morelos, their leaders dreamed of a free republic based on a wide distribution of property. However, there was little in the liberal creed, with its faith in private property and in elective democracy, to benefit the Indian peasants, who continued to live outside politics, labouring as peons on the *haciendas*, and regarding all white persons as their enemies. Liberal support came partly from a minority of radical Creole intellectuals, but mainly from the *mestizo* middle class – schoolmasters, minor civil servants, ranchers, small business men, and so on. Whereas the strength of the conservatives lay in the capital, where the wealthy people preferred to live, the liberals were stronger in the provinces; they tended to group themselves around local political bosses, or *caciques*, who wielded considerable power in their regions. Hence the liberal preference for a federal form of government, with a considerable degree of regional autonomy, as against the conservatives' more realistic desire for strong centralized control.

Cutting across these ideological divisions, and blurring their lines, there was a strong element of 'personalism' in Mexican politics, especially among the generals. The revolutionary leaders, such as Hidalgo, Morelos, Victoria and Guerrero, were no doubt genuine patriots, and fought, not for personal aggrandisement, but for what they believed. There can be little doubt too that, for example, Valentín Gómez Farías, a physician from Zacatecas, who led the liberal party for more than a quarter of a century, as also his principal conservative opponent, Lucas Alamán, the author of a classic history of Mexico, were men of integrity, who believed passionately in the very different doctrines which they preached. But these were rare and shining examples of virtue in an age when most of the generals and politicians were opportunist in their approach to politics, their personal ambition for the spoils of office being but thinly disguised behind the grandiloquent phrases of their 'Pronouncements' and 'Plans'.

General Antonio López de Santa Anna is the classic example of an unscrupulous but colourful soldier-politician, who managed with incredible agility to dominate the political scene during the first thirty-five years of the republic's history. Indeed the story of this troubled period of Mexican history can almost be told in terms of the ups and downs in the career of this remarkable man. Here are some of the highlights.

On *29 March, 1821* Santa Anna, who had made a good name for himself as a young officer in the Spanish Royalist army, carried out a successful dawn attack against the rebel army, which was supporting Iturbide. For his good services to the Spanish Crown he had been promoted to Lieutenant-Colonel on that very day. However, on the same afternoon he decided to change sides, and was rewarded by the rank of full colonel in the rebel army – two promotions in two opposing armies on one day!

On *1 December, 1822*, having sworn his undying loyalty to the Emperor, Iturbide, Santa Anna again changed sides; in Vera Cruz, he initiated the republican revolt which resulted in Guadalupe Victoria becoming the first President of Mexico. However, during the presidencies of Victoria (1824–28) and Guerrero (1828–29) he remained in the background politically, confining himself to military duties in Vera Cruz and Yucatán, or looking after his estate. Overshadowed by the heroes of the revolution, his time as a politician had not yet come.

In *1829*, the Spaniards, who still refused to recognize Mexico's independence, landed a force in Tampico. Santa Anna took charge of the Mexican troops, defeating the invaders, and becoming a national hero.

In *1830* Guerrero was driven from the presidency (he was captured and executed in the following year), and the conservative general,

Anastasio Bustamante, assumed dictatorial powers. In 1832, Santa Anna, aligning himself with the liberals, mounted a revolution which drove Bustamante from Mexico City. He was rewarded by being 'elected' President, with the liberal leader, Gómez Farías, as his Vice-President.

From *1832 to 1834*, having reached the political summit, Santa Anna, on the plea of ill-health, retired to his *hacienda* in Vera Cruz, leaving the government in the hands of Gómez Farías, as acting President. The latter proceeded to enact a whole series of anticlerical laws, which infuriated the conservative establishment. In 1834 Santa Anna, sensing the rising tide of discontent, suddenly changed sides once more, dismissed Gómez Farías from office, repealed the reform legislation, and governed the country as a dictator, under a new centralistic constitution. He was hailed by the conservatives, the Church and the army as the saviour of Mexico.

In *1835* Texas, which was still then a part of Mexico, rebelled. Santa Anna marched north, but after a bloodthirsty campaign of repression, was surprised and defeated by Sam Houston. He deserted his army, and was captured by the Texans dressed in civilian clothes and hiding in a clump of long grass. To save his life, he signed a humiliating agreement with his captors that, in return for his freedom, the Mexican forces would withdraw from Texas. On his return to Mexico in disgrace he retired to his *hacienda*, apparently a broken and discredited man. The colourless, but honest Anastasio Bustamante became President of Mexico for a second time.

In *1838* a French fleet, in an action known as the Pastry War, occupied Vera Cruz in an effort to collect some debts, one of them on behalf of a French baker whose premises had been destroyed by some unruly Mexican. Santa Anna took charge of the Mexican troops, and after a skirmish the French withdrew. In the action Santa Anna was wounded in the leg, and became once more a national hero. Subsequently, he arranged to have his amputated leg buried with honours in the Cathedral in Mexico City – a splendid example of his gift for showmanship and self-advertisement.

With his prestige restored, the wounded hero was inevitably sucked back into politics. Bustamante was overthrown in 1841. Santa Anna took over for a second time as a dictator, until he himself was overthrown in 1844, and retired to exile in Havana.

In *1845* Texas was admitted as a state by the USA, and war broke out between Mexico and her powerful northern neighbour. Santa Anna, after some very dubious private negotiations in Cuba with emissaries of President James K. Polk of the USA, was allowed to pass through the American maritime blockade and return to Mexico, where he took over the presidency from General Paredes and assumed command of the Mexican army. He fought an inconclusive battle with General Zachary Taylor in the north (which he subsequently claimed as a great victory); then he hurried south to meet General Winfield Scott, who had landed in Vera Cruz. In spite of a brave defence (in which Santa Anna appears quite genuinely to have distinguished himself) Mexico City was occupied by the Americans. In the subsequent peace treaty Mexico lost not only Texas, but California and all the territory lying north of the Rio Grande. Branded as a traitor by his political enemies,[3] Santa Anna retired into exile once more.

Having suffered enough under two successive liberal Presidents, Generals José Joaquin Herrera (1848–51) and Mariano Arista (1851–53), a combination of conservative and clerical forces overthrew Arista, and invited Santa Anna to return to Mexico to take charge of the government: in spite of all his past misdeeds, the conservatives could think of no better candidate. Thus for a glorious year Santa Anna, who now called himself 'His Most Serene Highness', ruled as a dictator with all the trappings of royalty. In 1854, however, the liberals counter-attacked, and in the following year, after an unsuccessful campaign against the rebels, Santa Anna retired into exile for the fourth time.

This was the end of the road, politically, for this remarkable man, who combined in his personality so many conflicting traits; real military ability combined with a love of showmanship; political shrewdness overlaid by immense vanity; great physical courage but with occasional acts of cowardice; kindness towards friends and cruelty towards enemies; a devoted husband but an inveterate womanizer; the look of a mournful philosopher, but a lover of cockfights and gambling; what appears to have been a genuine love of his country marred by occasional acts of betrayal. Yet, in spite of all his faults, Mexico could not do without Santa Anna for very long during those troubled thirty-five years. But now in 1855 his day was over. Mexican politics entered into a more serious phase. As for Santa Anna, the poor man lingered on as a forgotten figure from the past for twenty more years. His various attempts to stage a comeback were frustrated. Finally, in his old age, he was allowed to return to Mexico, where he died, blind and practically penniless, in 1876.

JUÁREZ AND THE LIBERAL 'REFORM'

Exit the colourful Santa Anna. Enter the grim, unsmiling liberal leader Benito Juárez, the son of an Indian peasant, who for the next twenty years occupied the centre of the Mexican stage.

No sooner had the new liberal government taken office – at first with the Indian guerrilla leader, Juan Álvarez, acting as President, and then, later in the same year, under the presidency of the more polished and moderate Ignacio Comonfort – than Juárez, now Minister of Justice, fired the first shot in the liberal campaign, with a decree abolishing the clerical and military *fueros*. In the following year Miguel Lerdo de Tejada, the Secretary of the Treasury, fired a second barrel with a law ordering that all the estates owned by the Church must be sold. The avowed purposes of this confiscatory legislation were to increase the revenue of the government and to stimulate economic progress by putting the Church's capital into circulation. But its social consequences for Mexico proved to be a mixed blessing. No provision was made for distributing the Church lands among the people who most needed them – the Indian peasants. Only rich men were able to pay the purchase price and sales tax on the Church's vast *haciendas*, with the result that a new class of wealthy landowners, many of them foreigners, was created, while the condition of the peasants got worse. For, as a sop to the clergy, the *Ley Lerdo* decreed that not only the Church, but all corporations of any kind were forbidden to own land – a provision which made it easier for the big landowners, by various tricks, to deprive the peasants of their land.

In 1857, a new liberal constitution was promulgated. It was a noble and inspiring document, but made little attempt to tackle the basic problems of the country, the poverty of the masses, illiteracy, class divisions, etc., being mainly concerned with establishing 'democratic' safeguards against clerical and military dictatorships, by compiling a long list of individual rights which no government was supposed to violate. The much-disputed abolition of religious and military *fueros*, and the prohibition of corporate ownership of land, were written into the constitution, together with a number of other measures calculated to infuriate the clergy; for example, monks were made free to retract from their vows. However, although there were fierce debates on the subject, the Congress balked at including an outright statement of religious freedom in the constitution.

The conservatives were filled with loathing of the liberal government and all its works. The Church retaliated by excommunicating all officials who took the oath to uphold the new constitution, and all persons who acquired the Church lands. In 1858, a section of the army revolted, and General Felix Zuloaga seized power in Mexico City. Comonfort, who as a 'moderate' had never had any stomach for the fight, departed into exile, and the unpopular 'Laws of the Reform' were repealed. Juárez, who escaped to Querétaro, was declared by the liberals to be the legitimate President, and proceeded to set up a rival government in Vera Cruz, while the conservatives, with their own President, held the City of Mexico. Three years of bitter civil war followed. Churches were stripped and gutted, and the sacred images and relics burnt on huge bonfires by marauding bands of guerrilla liberals. Priests who refused to administer the sacraments to the soldiers of the liberal armies were shot. But woe betide any liberals who fell into the hands of the ferocious conservative General, Leonardo Márquez, the Tiger of Tacubaya, who earned his nickname, not only by shooting all his prisoners, but by putting to death some unarmed medical students who had gone to the aid of the wounded in a defeated liberal army. At first the conservatives, who had some able generals and a more disciplined army, seemed to be winning the war, but in 1860 the tide turned and the guerrilla armies of the liberals closed in on Mexico City. In August, General Miguel Miramón, who had taken over the conservative presidency from General Zuloaga in 1858, took flight and went into exile. Early in 1861, the grim and indomitable Juárez, looking like an undertaker in his black civilian clothes, and seated in a hearse-like black carriage, drove into the capital in triumph.

But the conservatives still had a trump card up their sleeves – foreign intervention. As might be expected, the properties and interests of foreign merchants and investors had suffered a great deal of damage during the civil war. For example, in San Luis Potosí, a British-owned silver train worth more than a million pesos was confiscated by the liberals. Worse still, the conservative Miramón, desperate for money, raided the British Legation and appropriated seven hundred thousand pesos which had been set aside for the British bondholders. The French and the Spaniards had similar grievances, and a formidable list of claims. When Juárez returned to Mexico City he found the treasury empty, and decreed a suspension for two years on all foreign debts. In November 1861 the Mexican Congress rejected an agreement which Juárez had made with the British Minister, Sir Charles Wyke, under which British officials were to take over the administration of the Customs, as a means of protecting the interests of the foreign bondholders.

This was the last straw for Mexico's European creditors. With the Monroe Doctrine in temporary suspension because of the Civil War in the USA, a joint European force, consisting of Spanish, French and British detachments, landed in Vera Cruz in January 1862. To do it justice, the British Government, when agreeing to take part in this expedition, had made it clear to its allies that it was only interested in protecting British interests, and had no intention of interfering with the internal affairs of Mexico. But it soon became clear that the French had a more sinister design. Mexican conservative refugees in Paris had won the ear of the French Emperor, Napoleon III, and convinced that ambitious monarch that the only solution of Mexico's problem was for a European Prince to be put on the throne of Mexico with the help of the French army. A willing candidate for the Mexican crown had been found in the Archduke Maximilian, younger brother of the Hapsburg Emperor of Austria. In April, the British and Spaniards withdrew their forces from Vera Cruz, having achieved nothing. The French contingent was then reinforced and proceeded to march upon Mexico City. Having first suffered a serious defeat in Puebla on 5 May 1862 (this Mexican victory is now celebrated in Mexico as a national holiday), the French army succeeded in capturing Mexico City in the following year. Juárez fled to the north in order to carry on the struggle from bases close to the United States border, from which he could expect to receive generous supplies of American arms. After a faked plebiscite, carried out under the bayonets of the French army, Maximilian was formally offered the throne of Mexico, which he accepted, in the naïve belief that he would be welcomed with open arms by the grateful Mexicans.

It is difficult not to feel sorry for the unfortunate Maximilian and his wife Carlotta, who were duped by Napoleon into undertaking this crazy mission. Brought up in the secluded atmosphere of the

Austrian Court, the new Emperor of Mexico had no idea of the depth of the hatred which divided his adopted people; he seemed to think that it would only need a few good parties in his palace – on the ship coming out he wrote a voluminous book on court etiquette, and upon his arrival launched himself into a tremendous social round – to bring the Mexican family together again. But his tentative peace feeler to Juárez was rejected with contempt. And it was not long before he had fallen out with his conservative and clerical backers, when he refused outright to restore to the Church the land which had been sold. To their astonishment and chagrin the conservatives began to realize that Maximilian was a bit of a liberal in a gentlemanly kind of way. Meanwhile his French backers were only interested in collecting financial claims (to which was now added the bill for the cost of the occupying army) from an empty Mexican imperial treasury. In 1865, the American Civil War came to an end, and Seward, the United States Secretary of State, began pressing Napoleon for evacuation, while stepping up the supply of arms to Juárez. The Mexican adventure had become unpopular in France, and anyhow the French army was now urgently needed at home to meet the growing threat of Bismarck's Prussia. And so the distasteful decision was taken by Napoleon to desert Maximilian. Carlotta hurried back to Europe to plead with the French Emperor and the Pope, and went mad while on her visit to the Vatican. Maximilian dithered, retiring to Jalapa, where he spent his time hunting tropical butterflies; but finally he reached the brave, but rash, decision to remain in Mexico at the head of his now beleaguered troops. The end was tragic. In 1867, the imperial army was defeated outside Querétaro, and Maximilian and his two principal generals, Miramón and Mejía, were captured. The three men were sentenced by a military court to be executed. Requests for a pardon poured in from the courts of Europe, but Juárez was adamant.[4] On 19 June, Maximilian, Miramón and Mejía were lined up against a wall and shot.

After the downfall of Maximilian, Juárez ruled Mexico as a constitutional president – the first civilian president Mexico had ever had – until 1872 when he was struck down by a heart attack. He inherited a deplorable situation. The treasury was empty; the internal debt had reached the staggering sum of three hundred million pesos; and the roads were infested by bandits. In 1869, to add to his troubles, there was a terrible drought and widespread famine. However,

79

under his honest and methodical management, and in spite of his difficulties with a recalcitrant Congress – for he remained a dedicated democrat to the end – the country at length turned the corner and began to recover.

In Mexico today (except in right-wing Roman Catholic circles) Juárez, along with Hidalgo and Morelos, is regarded as one of the great heroes and benefactors of the republic, and a precursor of the Mexican Revolution. He was certainly a man of great integrity, and his achievements were impressive. By breaking the political and economic power of the Roman Catholic Church, he destroyed one of the main props of the nineteenth-century Mexican establishment. If it did not help the Indians, the national economy was to benefit greatly in the long run by the forced sale of the Church's great estates; public education, which Juárez fostered assiduously, was freed from clerical control. Perhaps most important, by defying the French invaders and unseating Maximilian, Juárez succeeded in identifying the cause of reform with that of national independence, and became the symbol, not only of a liberal constitution, but also of a nation. As for the constitution, the future would reveal its essential weakness (Mexico could not do without a strong, centralized government), but it was of lasting importance in spelling out so clearly what ought to be the basic rights of the individual citizen – equality under the law, the right to vote, the responsibility of the State for public education – even if the country was not yet ready to turn these abstractions into reality.

Where the liberal reform movement failed was in not doing anything (except on paper) to rescue the Indian peasants from the bondage of peonage or to break up the great landed estates. In social and economic outlook the Mexican liberal political philosophy was essentially bourgeois, representing the interests, not so much of the mass of the people, as of the new and rising *mestizo* middle class. Meanwhile, although the prop of the Church had been weakened, two strong pillars of the conservative establishment had remained intact. The landowning oligarchy had, if anything, grown more powerful with the acquisition of Church lands. Although the constitution had removed some of its privileges, the army, too, remained, as it had always been, the final arbiter of politics. Once Juárez had gone it soon became apparent that there was no civilian politician of sufficient authority to keep the generals under control.

In 1876 democracy gave up the ghost, and for the next thirty-five years Mexico experienced, under Porfirio Díaz, the longest and most absolute military dictatorship in her history. The democratic system of government, for which the liberals had fought so passionately, survived only on paper, representing a hope for the future, but with little or no substance in reality.

6   The Porfirian dictatorship

PORFIRIO DÍAZ, like Juárez, was a man of humble origin. With only
a smattering of education, he came up in the world the hard way
through the ranks of the guerrilla armies during the War of the
Reform. The most successful of the liberal generals, it was Díaz who
led the conquering army of the Reform into Mexico City upon the
downfall of Maximilian in 1867. The jubilant commander made
elaborate preparations to celebrate the triumphal return of Juárez,
which he had done so much to bring about. But the civilian Juárez
did not like soldiers, and cold-shouldered Díaz. Worse still, Juárez
proceeded forthwith to disband two-thirds of the army, with hardly
a word of thanks to the troops and no pensions. Bitterly offended,
and determined upon revenge, Díaz resigned his commission in the
army, and retired to his sugar estate in Oaxaca, which had been
presented to him by the grateful citizens of his native state.

In 1871 Díaz ran as a candidate against Juárez, who was bidding
for a fourth term in the presidency. But in the three-cornered struggle
which ensued – Sebastián Lerdo de Tejada, a leading liberal politician, had also entered the lists – none of the candidates secured a
majority. The choice devolved on Congress, which elected Juárez as
president, and appointed Lerdo as president of the Supreme Court.
Left out in the cold, Díaz attempted to seize Mexico City by force, but
his revolt failed. Disguised as a priest, he fled into hiding in the
mountains of Nayarit, where a friendly Indian chieftain offered him
protection.

Lerdo succeeded Juárez in the presidency in 1872. But, although a
highly cultured man, he lacked the political skill and authority of
his old master. Thus when, in 1876, he announced his intention of
standing for a second term, the country was ripe for a revolution.
Díaz, this time disguised as a Cuban doctor, slipped ashore in Vera

Cruz, and made his way to his native state of Oaxaca where he organized an army. On 21 November he entered Mexico City in triumph and took over the presidency.

'BREAD OR THE STICK'

As a liberal, Díaz had fought for the establishment of democratic government, but as a disillusioned soldier he had come to believe that democracy would never work in Mexico. Even Juárez, the most determined of democrats, had found it exceedingly difficult to govern effectively, faced as he was by a recalcitrant and often irresponsible Congress, and rebellious provincial *caciques* (many of them former guerrilla leaders), who wielded great political power in their own regions and paid scant attention to the dictates of the central government. Díaz was determined to suffer no 'democratic nonsense' from any quarter. There was only room, he believed, for one *cacique* in Mexico, the President of the Republic, and this was the role he intended to play.

Díaz consolidated his position as an all-powerful president by employing the time-honoured dictatorial technique of *Pan o Palo* (bread or the stick). Whatever may have been their political affiliations in the past, liberals as well as former imperialists were recruited into the ranks of his supporters by being offered not only jobs in the bureaucracy and the army, but also plenty of opportunities for making money on the side. Díaz himself was scrupulously honest in his personal financial affairs, as also were some of his closest advisers; but the dictator had a blind eye for the graft and peculation of his state governors and generals, some of whom were little better than racketeers. For example, in Puebla, General Mucio Martínez, governor for eighteen years, became a millionaire by owning a dozen gambling houses (although gambling was prohibited by law), and holding the monopoly in his state for the sale of pulque, an intoxicating drink extracted from the maguey cactus which was very popular with the Indians. Luis Torres, in Sonora, made a fortune, first by selling arms to the Yaqui Indians in his territory, and thus encouraging them to revolt; then, having put down the rebellion, by selling the Indians into slavery to the henequen growers in Yucatán for so much a head.[1]

But if his officials and generals in the provinces were allowed to grow rich, they were never allowed to grow too powerful. To keep his supporters under control Díaz would constantly shift his support from one man to another, so balancing his appointments that the too powerful state governor would find himself supervised by a local army commander who was loyal to Díaz, or vice versa. With political enemies the dictator was ruthless. For his opponents there were no jobs, no favours and no lucrative rackets. They would be lucky if they were not imprisoned or shot. The press, which had been free under Juárez, was likewise gagged. The editor who criticized the regime went in danger of his life. Friendly newspapers on the other hand were subsidized. Thus the Mexican press degenerated into an obedient and laudatory claque.

By these methods Díaz succeeded in obtaining the almost unanimous support both of the old conservative establishment of landowners, army and Church, and the new *mestizo* middle class. For the oligarchy this was a golden age, with plenty of opportunities to make money. The generals, who in the past had caused most of the revolutionary troubles, were persuaded to become pillars of the dictatorship by being paid their salaries regularly, with the chance also of making some extra money on the side. Towards the Roman Catholic Church, Díaz, while retaining the liberal anticlerical laws in the statute book, was benevolently lenient; he shut his eyes to infringements against the law which prevented the Church from owning property. Through nominees and other subterfuges, the Church was allowed by Díaz to re-acquire a good deal of property, although never to the extent of obtaining its old stranglehold over the economic life of the nation. In this policy of appeasement Díaz was no doubt influenced by his wife, Carmen, a devout Roman Catholic and a member of a leading aristocratic family. His policy paid off handsomely in political terms by healing (on the surface at any rate) the old religious quarrel between liberals and conservatives, thus uniting the oligarchy and the middle class behind the dictatorship. As for the middle class, this segment of the population, too, had never before had it so good. A greatly expanded bureaucracy offered plenty of jobs. With the economic expansion of the country there was ample scope for the small farmer, rancher or business man. The educational opportunities improved as large numbers of schools were built, mainly in the towns. By 1910, according to the official statistics, Mexico had some twelve thousand schools, with an attendance of about nine hundred thousand. But it was middle class pupils who were the principal beneficiaries.[2]

Thus Mexico, under Díaz, became a happy family; but with one important omission – the Indians. However, apart from a few radicals, nobody at this time in Mexico bothered their heads very much about mere Indian peasants, whom most educated Mexicans, whether white or *mestizo*, regarded as belonging to an inferior race. Díaz was determined to modernize the country by developing its economic resources. For this purpose foreign capital had to be attracted. And what better way could there be of attracting the foreign investor than by keeping the peasants and the industrial workers firmly in their place, so that there would be an ample supply of cheap and docile labour? Thus for these unprivileged segments of the population the ration of 'bread' was kept down to the minimum, while the 'stick' was applied mercilessly to the back of any Indian who did not behave himself.

By these arbitrary methods Díaz pacified a country which had been torn apart by faction and civil war for most of the time since independence. The bandits disappeared from the roads, the budget was balanced, and a settlement reached with the British bondholders. Mexico became a paradise for foreign investors. The price paid by the Mexicans for these tremendous advantages was the almost total loss of their civil liberties. As national *cacique*, Díaz controlled all appointments, both of officials and of national and state congressmen. The legislature and the judiciary became rubber stamps. Elections were a farce. When his first term of office expired in 1880, Díaz, who had based his original political campaign on the slogan 'effective suffrage and no re-election', found himself faced with the problem of selecting a successor, who could be trusted to keep the presidential seat warm for him. He found the perfect stooge in General Manuel González, an old army friend, who occupied the presidency until 1884, when Díaz was once again 'elected' to this high office. After this interlude – it was one of scandalously corrupt government – Díaz conveniently forgot about the principle of no re-election, and thereafter ruled as a dictator (with occasional rigged elections) until finally forced to retire from the presidency in 1911.

ECONOMIC POLICY

When Díaz took over the presidency in 1876 Mexico was a bad word in the great financial centres of the world, but by the time he left office in 1911, the national income had been increased from some

$20 million to $100 million. There was a budget surplus of $136 million; exports had quintupled; imports had increased eight times; some 15,000 miles of railways and a number of modern ports had been built; gold and silver mining had increased from $25 million to $160 million; a whole range of new industries had been established; and, perhaps the greatest miracle of all, bearing in mind their past record of default, Mexican bonds stood at 97 on the London stock exchange and yielded less than 4 per cent.

Of all these various developments perhaps the most important for the future of the country was the building of the railways. The British-owned Mexican Railway Co. Ltd. was the first in the field, having been formed in London as long ago as 1863 to construct a line between the port of Vera Cruz and Mexico City. But owing to the revolutionary troubles it was not completed until 1872. This line, which climbed from sea-level to 7,500 feet above the ocean, was a magnificent engineering achievement, but it served only a very small part of the country.

In the north, as the new American railways drew close to the Mexican border, American capitalists began casting their gaze southwards, in search of new sources of freight and raw materials, to what seemed to be a land of almost unlimited potentialities. Lerdo, when he was President, had refused to grant concessions to American railroad companies to extend their lines down into Mexico, preferring to leave the desert of the north in its virgin state to serve as a *cordon sanitaire* between Mexico and her powerful northern neighbour. But Díaz was not prepared to allow his countrymen to indulge any longer in the luxury of xenophobia. He saw clearly that Mexico could not do without north-south railways connecting the country with the rich markets of the United States of America. In 1880 he granted three major concessions for the construction of railways connecting Mexico City with various points on the US border, and, with remarkable speed, these lines were duly built.

In 1889 the Mexican government entered into a deed of partnership with the British firm of S. Pearson and Co. to build a railway across the narrow Isthmus of Tehuantepec, and thus provide a short overland route of only 140 miles between the Gulf of Mexico and the Pacific Ocean. Weetman Pearson (later the first Lord Cowdray), a close friend of Díaz, had already proved his capability 'to deliver the goods' in such feats of engineering as the draining of the Valley of Mexico and the construction of Vera Cruz harbour – tasks in which earlier contractors of different nationalities had lamentably failed.

The difficulties which faced Pearson's engineers were immense. The Isthmus is a wild and densely forested region in which the temperature sometimes rises to 98°, while the rainfall on the Gulf side amounts to 123 inches, as much as 24 inches falling in a single month. Further, the district is frequently shaken by earthquakes. Indian labour, to the number of some 5,000 workmen, was recruited from the neighbouring hills, but among these hardy mountaineers, as also among the European staff, the death toll was heavy from yellow fever and other tropical diseases. Tough problems, too, were presented by the construction of the two terminal ports. The Gulf side offered fewer difficulties than the Pacific. A channel was cut through the bar of the Coatzacoatl river, and long stone breakwaters were built out from the entrance of the river to form a bottleneck, through which the stream rushed, keeping the channel permanently dredged by its scouring action. Along the side of the river, where there had previously been only a fishing village, were constructed wharves and warehouses fitted up in the most modern manner for the rapid handling of cargoes. But on the Pacific side there was no river to simplify the task of the engineers. At Salina Cruz there existed merely a dangerous open bay, in which an entirely artificial harbour was created by building great stone breakwaters, so as to enclose an inner harbour. This port was also provided with all the latest devices, including a graving dock which in its time was reputed to be the finest of its kind on the Pacific coast of America.

At length the great work was completed, the railway and the two ports being inaugurated with much pomp and ceremony in 1907. Pearson's optimism was justified by immediate results. He organized shipping services between ports on the North Atlantic seaboard of America and Coatzacoalcos, which ran in conjunction with ships on the Pacific, plying between Salina Cruz and California and the South Sea Islands. There thus developed a brisk traffic across the railway in sugar from Hawaii, canned goods from California, and other commodities. The figures speak for themselves. In 1909 the railway carried 699,000 tons of merchandise, which figure by 1911 had grown to 1,628,000 tons. Both Pearson and the Mexican government began to reap the benefits of their joint enterprise in the shape of substantial profits.[3]

Starting with less than 700 miles of track in 1880, Mexico possessed over 12,000 miles of line by 1910, with connections between most of the major cities; a line extended south to Guatemala, and there were no less than seven points of entry into Mexico by rail on the US border. Towards the end of his period in office, Díaz created a Mexican company, the National Railways of Mexico, in which the Mexican government was the major shareholder, to absorb about 60 per cent of the railway network. Today, partly through expropriation in 1937 and subsequent government purchases in 1946 and 1950, practically all the railways of Mexico are owned by the nation.

Side by side with the building of the railways, there were major developments of local industry in such fields as textiles, tobacco, beer, refined sugar, jute, wool, silk, paper, soap, canned meat, iron and steel, financed by both foreign and domestic capital. At the beginning of the new century oil was discovered in the region of Tampico and in the south, and its exploitation was undertaken by United States and British interests, to their subsequent great profit, but not without some considerable initial risks.

For example, in 1901, Pearson moved into oil. His engineers, while building the railway, had reported the existence of seepages of oil in various parts of the Isthmus. Test wells were sunk, and finally at San Cristobal, oil was duly struck. By 1907 Pearson had invested more than a million pounds of his own money in this oil venture, but he was still by no means out of the wood. In 1908 his rich well at Dos Bocas in the Tampico-Tuxpan region caught fire and burned steadily for eight weeks. Nearly one million tons of oil were lost. The turning point in Pearson's fortunes came in 1910 with the drilling of the well called Potrero No. 4. The technique of drilling was not then what it is now, and this 'gusher' could not be brought under control for a period of sixty days – two long months of perpetual anxiety, with the escaping oil and gas rising into the air in a great column and running away to waste at the rate of 100,000 barrels a day. It is estimated that some six million barrels were lost in this way. But the engineers – and Pearson himself rushed to the scene of the disaster – rose to the occasion, inventing on the spot a device, now known as the Bell nipple, by means of which the spurting oil was brought under control. By engaging in this risky venture, Pearson laid the foundations of the Cowdray fortune. But in 1938 his creation, the British-owned Mexican Eagle Oil Co., along with all the rest of the Mexican oil industry, until then mostly controlled by American companies, was expropriated by the Mexican government, so that oil, like the railways, is now a part of the national patrimony (see below, pp. 114–17).

There are many modern critics of Díaz who accuse him of having 'sold his country' to foreigners, with little regard to the interests of his own people. In fairness, however, it must be remembered that the nineteenth century was a tough world for underdeveloped countries; nobody then had ever heard of 'foreign aid'; foreign investors demanded security and the promise of a good return on their money. This Díaz was determined to provide. By 1910 the North American investment in Mexico – in railways, mines, cattle ranches, plantations and oil – amounted to more than a billion dollars. British, French and Spanish investments were likewise considerable. A few fortunate Mexicans profited greatly from these foreign ventures, as middlemen, lawyers etc., but the majority of the people began to feel as though they had become second-class citizens in their own country. These feelings of outraged national dignity found their expression in the explosion of the Mexican Revolution which followed the downfall of Díaz, and much of the dictator's good work of economic rehabilitation was swept away in the storm. But at least the essential infrastructure – the railways, public utilities, oilfields and factories – survived to the ultimate benefit of the Mexican people.

AGRICULTURE

The agricultural policy of Díaz, while beneficial in some ways, is also very much open to criticism. The liberals, following in the tradition of Morelos, had envisaged the creation of a nation of small individual landowners; but, as we saw, the *Ley Lerdo* had resulted in the concentration of land in larger units. Díaz now compounded this mistake by trying to superimpose modern capitalism upon the archaic feudal system of the *hacienda*. With the worthy object of making use of the national land, much of which was uncultivated, a survey was undertaken, with generous terms offered to the companies (many of them foreign) which were given concessions to carry out this work. Within nine years various companies surveyed almost 100 million acres of so-called vacant lands, of which over 30 million acres went to the surveyors, and another 40 million to private individuals and companies. In this process of land distribution there was a good deal

89

of graft by local officials, the land of many small isolated Indian communities being declared 'vacant' and swallowed up by the companies. By the end of Díaz's dictatorship the government had divested itself of an area roughly equal to that of California, mostly in the extreme north and south of the country. The new landowners, many of them organized in foreign companies, were essentially capitalistic entrepreneurs, and ran their estates, whether devoted to raising cattle or producing export crops such as henequen, sugar or rubber, efficiently. To this extent, therefore, the agricultural policy of Díaz can be said to have had a useful economic result.

But on the central plateau, the old traditional type of Mexican landowner continued to hold sway in the *haciendas*. On such estates the methods of agriculture were primitive and much of the land was wasted; for the old-style members of the oligarchy regarded their land as a badge of nobility and a source of power rather than as a business enterprise. Even so, if it suited their interests, they were just as greedy as the new companies in gobbling up the land of neighbouring villages and forcing the peasants into the servitude of peonage. Since the landowners usually had the local officials in their pocket, it was easy to outwit the simple peasants, who, if they protested, could expect nothing but the harshest treatment at the hands of the rural police. Díaz, himself an Indian, was not unsympathetic towards the plight of the peasants and occasionally intervened to protect them. But with such poor communications, it was the local officials who ruled the roost in the depth of the country, and from these petty tyrants the Indians could expect no mercy. By 1910 nearly half of Mexico belonged to less than three thousand families, while of the ten million Mexicans engaged in agriculture more than nine and a half million were virtually without land. Many of the estates were of enormous size. For example, Luis Terrazas in Chihuahua owned nearly five million acres of land. At the other end of the scale Indians, using the most primitive methods, cultivated minute plots of land from which they could barely make a living.

Thus agriculture under Díaz was a mixture of the efficient and the inefficient, the modern and the archaic, *latifundia* (huge estates) and *minifundia* (holdings too small to be viable). Rather curiously – since dictators are usually good at such things – Díaz did little to develop irrigation, or to build roads to act as feeders from the farms to the new railways. Potentially important agricultural areas were left

90

without communications and a market for their produce. Thus the increase in agricultural production, slightly more than 21 per cent between 1877 and 1907, was disappointing, during a time when the population increased by nearly 40 per cent. With the new emphasis on exports – sugar, coffee, henequen, beef etc. – the relative proportion of home-grown food declined, so that in the later years of the dictatorship essential food had to be imported. Between 1890 and 1910 the price of almost every important article of food was more than doubled. In 1910 the real wages of the peon, as measured by the price of maize, was one quarter of what it had been in 1800.[4]

PORFIRIAN SOCIETY

When in September 1910 Mexico celebrated the centenary of the *Grito de Dolores* (p. 66), delegations from all over the world flocked to the Mexican capital, to return home with nothing but praise for the prosperity and stability of the country, and for the dignified old man, now close on eighty years of age, who for thirty-five years had been the father of his people. Very few of the visiting foreign dignitaries – diplomats, journalists and business men, or even the intellectuals of this time – saw the cracks in the edifice on which modern scholarship, armed with the powerful weapon of hindsight, now tends to dwell. To the student in 1970 the Porfirian dictatorship can be seen, with all its many defects, as the prelude to the Mexican Revolution – as the last straw in a huge load of iniquities dating from colonial times which caused the overburdened and ill-treated camel finally to rebel. But in 1910 the intelligent observer, unable to look into the future, and aware only of the stormy and unhappy history of the republic, was amazed to find that so much had been achieved by Mexico in such a short time.

Order instead of chaos; railways in place of the old rutted and bandit-infested highways; new factories on every side; Mexico City looking like a little Paris with its fine tree-lined boulevard, the Paseo de la Reforma, and the marble splendour of the new opera house – no wonder that the delegates, as they sipped their champagne, were enchanted by everything they saw. True, from the carriage windows of the train, it was possible to observe the Indian peasants toiling in the fields as they had done since time immemorial; but this was surely to be expected in a country of Indian background which only a century ago had been a colony of Spain.

Mexican society was still oligarchical in structure, but its character had changed under Díaz in a number of important ways. The oligarchy had been not only expanded by recruits from the up-and-coming middle class, but revitalized by the entry into its ranks of the new industrial entrepreneurs. The traditional Spanish nobleman's disdain for work and business, which had characterized the old Mexican ruling class, had become outmoded by the go-ahead philosophy of positivism. Díaz increasingly came under the influence of a small and select group of highly able lawyers and intellectuals, nicknamed the '*científicos*', who were disciples of Auguste Comte and Herbert Spencer, and believed in the scientific, rather than the humanitarian, approach to social and political problems. The liberals had believed in democracy and social justice. The positivists believed in material progress, to achieve which everything else must be subordinated. The Indians, in their primitive barbarism, were an obstacle to progress. Rather than allow them to linger on in their outmoded village communities, they must be made to take their place in the economic life of the country as peons in the new efficient *haciendas* and workers in the factories; if they showed reluctance, they must be coerced along the path of civilization. As for democracy, it had been a failure in Mexico. Government must be made honest, efficient and scientific; it was thus best entrusted to the hands of the educated white elite. Only so, it was argued, could Mexico hope to enter into the modern world.

In accordance with these doctrines, the government of Díaz, which had originally been rooted in the native soil of the *mestizo* middle class, as represented by the old-guard liberal provincial *caciques* and the veterans of the war of Reform, became increasingly the preserve of a small, highly sophisticated clique of rich white men – men of cultivated taste who could hold their own in a drawing room any-where in the world, but were almost like foreigners in their own country, and lacked the common touch. The *científicos* looked to Paris, London and New York for ideas and inspiration, and disdained their own people and country. For example, the historian Francisco Bulnes, a leading member of the ruling clique, seemed positively to delight in denigrating Mexico's past, and poking fun at her national heroes. Mexican art and literature of this period slavishly copied European models; the same went for sculpture and architecture. In the houses of wealthy Mexicans the ladies sipped tea in drawing rooms furnished in the style of Louis XV. There were many rich Mexicans, drawing ample revenues from their landed estates, who preferred to live in Paris, rather than in their own country, and spoke Spanish with an affected French accent. It became fashionable for Mexican boys of the upper class to be sent to England to get their schooling at the Jesuit college of Stoneyhurst.

Many of the leaders in this group were men of ability and integrity; for example José Limantour did a splendid job in putting Mexico's finances on to a sound basis. But the *científicos*, together with the foreign capitalists with whom they were so closely associated, became extremely unpopular among the general run of Mexicans. These feelings of resentment came to a head when Francisco Madero, a wealthy landowner of liberal leanings, raised the standard of revolt against Díaz in 1911. At the beginning the Mexican Revolution was not so much the popular revolt of downtrodden peasants and workers, into which it developed later, as a movement by the Mexican middle class to rid itself of the hated clique of rich Mexicans and foreigners who had managed to capture the ear of Díaz and dictate his policies.

Not that the peasants and workers were lacking in grievances. As a result of the agricultural policy of Díaz the peasants, as we saw, were increasingly divested of their land and forced into peonage; meanwhile their standard of living declined as a result of rising prices of basic foods. As for the workers, the conditions in the mines and factories were appalling. During the last decade of the dictatorship the first trade unions were formed. A few brave spirits, such as Ricardo and Enrique Flores Magón, began to preach socialism, while Spanish immigrants introduced the doctrines of anarcho-syndicalism. But strikes and disorders were dealt with harshly. For example, at the American-owned copper mines at Cananea in Sonora and in the textile mills of Rio Blanco in Vera Cruz Mexican troops shot down in cold blood hundreds of unarmed workers who dared to lift up their voices in protest.

By such cruel measures Díaz gave Mexico thirty-five years of enforced peace, and laid some of the economic foundations of her present-day prosperity, but he did little or nothing to solve the nation's political and social problems. The deep-seated social divisions in society, the poverty of the masses, peonage and sweated labour in the factories – all these evil inheritances from the colonial past were intensified rather than ameliorated under Díaz. Meanwhile the slender democratic plant which the liberals had tried unsuccessfully to cultivate withered and died. However, to blame Díaz for what were the shortcomings of his day and age, to blame him in effect for having failed to anticipate the Mexican Revolution, would be rather like critizing the aged Duke of Wellington, when he was Prime Minister, for not having introduced the Reform Bill, with the Lloyd George budget thrown in for good measure. In Britain six hundred years of social and political evolution elapsed between Magna Carta and the first Reform bill; a further one hundred years were needed for the industrial revolution, with its attendant evils of slums and sweated labour, to produce the modern welfare state. In contrast, Mexico in 1910 had had only one hundred years of experience as an independent republic, and her industrial revolution had only just begun. Still essentially a peasant society, her deep-seated problems of economic underdevelopment and racial and cultural integration had no parallel in Europe or North America.

7 The Mexican Revolution

IT WAS NO ORDINARY REVOLUTION, such as had so frequently punctuated Mexican history in the past, that was set in motion when the mild little idealist, Francisco Madero, on 5 October 1910, issued his challenge to the mighty Díaz. The revolution which ensued (known as the Mexican Revolution) not only got rid of Díaz, but after some ten years of chaos set in motion the process of political, social and economic change which, during the last sixty years, has gone a long way towards transforming Mexico into a modern state. With Madero's uprising the modern history of the country began.

Madero came from a wealthy family which owned *haciendas*, cotton plantations and smelting plants in the northern border state of Coahuila. But, although brought up in comfortable circumstances, he was a man of high ideals who suffered from a tender social conscience; early on in his career he had shocked his more hard-headed relatives by the lavish social benefits which he showered on the workers in the family cotton estate which had been entrusted to his care. But although humanitarian in his instincts, he was very far from being revolutionary in his political outlook; it was never a part of his political philosophy to seek to bring about a radical transformation of society. His first political tract, a book published in 1908 entitled *The Presidential Succession of 1910*, was essentially no more than a plea for a return to the democratic spirit of the liberal Constitution of 1857. With Díaz now an old man, it was time, Madero argued, for the people to assert themselves in the matter of choosing his successor. Madero was sufficiently a realist, however, to accept that the elderly Díaz should be allowed to continue in the presidency for yet another term, asking only that the electorate in 1910 should be permitted to exercise their free choice in selecting the vice-president, as a first step towards the re-establishment of democracy.

A man of peace and good will, Madero paid a friendly call on Díaz in order to explain his political ideas. But the dictator just could not take this earnest little man seriously. It was a grave misjudgement. When Díaz made it clear that he intended not only to stand himself as president, but at the same time 'impose' the unpopular Ramón Corral as vice-president for a second term, Madero took the bold step of announcing himself as a presidential candidate in opposition to Díaz. Adopting Díaz's own slogan, with which the dictator had first won power but since betrayed, 'Effective Suffrage, no Re-election', clubs were formed all over the country to support Madero's campaign.

Observing with surprise and alarm the evident popularity of the opposition candidate, Díaz took the precaution of casting Madero into jail just before the elections took place in July 1910. Thus the now habitual farce of a manipulated election was repeated, a vast majority of the votes being claimed for Díaz, and with only a token 196 votes allotted to Madero. Feeling once more secure on his throne, Díaz then allowed Madero to be released from prison. But the dictator had underrated his adversary. Taking refuge in the USA, Madero on 5 October 1910 issued a manifesto, known as the *Plan of San Luis Potosí*, denouncing the faked elections, naming himself provisional president, and calling upon the people to revolt against Díaz. A date, 20 November 1910, was set for the uprising. Forewarned, the government struck first on 16 November, making numerous arrests. There followed a number of unco-ordinated rebellions in different parts of the country which were quickly crushed. Madero, who had crossed the Mexican border to lead the revolutionary forces, found himself with nobody to lead and returned dejectedly to his exile in the USA. The British Minister's first telegram from Mexico City reporting the outbreak was dated 19 November and was dismissed in the Foreign Office with the cryptic minute 'hardly worth reporting by telegram'. A week later the British Legation reported that the trouble seemed to be over, with the government in firm control of the situation. Such was the inauspicious beginning of the Mexican Revolution.[1]

But the trouble was very far from over. A few days later the telegraph wires were throbbing with the news of a more serious uprising in the northern state of Chihuahua led by an obscure small-town storekeeper, Pascual Orozco, and a disgruntled ranch hand, Pancho Villa. The latter after a quarrel with his master (his sister had been raped by the landowner's son), had taken to the hills and become an outlaw. In this wide open cattle country, it was not difficult for these two determined men to organize an army of hard-riding cowboys who, by attacking the key points on the railways, were able to outwit the federal troops and gain control of the state. Taking heart once more, Madero hastened to join forces with the rebels. Moreover, as the news of these developments spread, the whole country began to take fire, with local uprisings in practically every state. In Morelos, for example, the grim and taciturn peasant leader, Emiliano Zapata, emerged from obscurity to become the legendary leader of an army of white-clad *campesinos* which began systematically to burn and loot the rich sugar estates of this region. Taking alarm, the US Government massed troops along the Mexican border so as to be able to intervene if necessary to protect American lives and property.

Limantour, who had temporarily fallen out of favour with Díaz, rushed back from Europe at the bidding of his old master and initiated negotiations with Madero and his principal political lieutenant, Francisco Vásquez Gómez. But the revolutionaries, in no mood now for compromise, demanded the resignation of Díaz and the expulsion of the hated *científicos* from Congress. On 21 May the representatives of the government accepted Madero's terms, and a peace treaty was signed by which it was agreed to establish a provisional government under the former Mexican ambassador in Washington, Francisco León de la Barra, pending the holding of free elections, from which it was confidently expected that Madero, now at the height of his popularity, would emerge as the victor. But the aged dictator, stubborn to the last, refused to yield. It was not until his palace guard had fired upon an angry crowd outside his house shouting for his resignation, that the old man, in agony from an abscessed tooth, gave way in the early morning of 25 May. On the next day, with the connivance of two of Pearson's British aides, he was smuggled out of the capital on the British-owned Interoceanic Railway and put on a ship in Vera Cruz which was bound for Europe. Shortly before he died in Paris on 2 July 1915, during a time when Mexico was still rent assunder by civil war, an unrepentant Díaz remarked to a reporter in justification of his dictatorial policy, 'I knew my Mexico'. At the time when these words were uttered it looked as though he had been right.

THE STRUGGLE FOR LEADERSHIP (1911–1916)

Madero, it soon transpired, was not a strong enough man to control or guide the tremendous forces which his successful rebellion had unloosed. No sooner had the provisional president, de la Barra, taken his seat than the supporters of Madero found themselves engaged in deadly combat within the Government and Congress with former members of the Porfirian oligarchy, who were busily seeking to re-establish a basis of power within the new regime. Meanwhile on the left of the revolutionary movement the guerrilla leaders refused to disband their private armies; Zapata's peasants continued to attack and occupy the land of the *haciendas*; the workers began to organize themselves into trade unions; the politicians in Congress indulged themselves in the unaccustomed luxury of free debate; and the intellectuals were busy drawing up utopian blueprints. None of this revolutionary activity was at all good for business, and both the local and foreign business men were filled with gloom. The Revolution had let loose repressed feelings of nationalism which found expression in the public statements of the revolutionary leaders, although Madero himself was very far from being unfriendly to foreign capital. Even so, the foreign capitalists, who had had it so good under Porfirio Díaz, took alarm and angrily demanded the protection of their governments. With the United States ambassador, Henry Lane Wilson, sending a stream of alarmist reports to Washington (the British Legation was much more phlegmatic), there was a real danger that, unless order could be quickly restored, the United States might be tempted to intervene.

Madero, who was duly elected President by an overwhelming majority of votes and took office in November 1911, showed very quickly that he was incapable of providing the strong government which both the local and foreign capitalists had come to expect from the chief executive of the Mexican Republic. A sincere democrat, Madero allowed the new popularly-elected Congress to have its head in a country which had had hitherto only a disappointing experience of parliamentary government. In spite of his humanitarian philosophy, Madero's government had no properly worked-out programme of social reform to offer to the people, nor did it have any agrarian policy beyond some vague expressions of concern for the plight of the peasants. Madero tried, but failed, to come to terms with Zapata who continued his relentless war against the *haciendas*. In his 'Plan of Ayala', in open defiance of Madero, Zapata called for the immediate restoration of lands taken from the peasants, and in addition for the seizure of one-third of the lands of the *haciendas*. In the Congress, the radical leader, Luis Cabrera, was likewise vociferously demanding a drastic programme of agrarian reform. But Madero, very much under the influence of his brother Gustavo and his other wealthy relatives, and no doubt acutely conscious of the need to allay the fears of the US ambassador, took little positive action on the agrarian front.

Increasingly the radicals lost confidence in Madero as a revolutionary leader, while the conservative business and army leaders began to despise him for his weakness. The inevitable revolts followed. On the left, declaring that he had betrayed the Revolution, Madero's former supporter, Pascual Orozco, rose against him in Chihuahua and was only crushed after an arduous campaign led by Madero's best general, Victoriano Huerta. Meanwhile, Zapata's revolutionary forces continued to elude the Federal troops in Morelos. Representing the right wing in politics, Bernardo Reyes led an abortive revolt in the north, but it was a fiasco and he ended up in prison. The same fate awaited Felix Díaz (a nephew of Don Porfirio) who 'pronounced' against the government in Vera Cruz. However, on Sunday 9 February 1913 the troops at Tacubaya on the outskirts of Mexico City revolted and Reyes and Díaz were released from prison. Reyes then led an attack upon the national palace, but was killed by the guards, whereupon Felix Díaz retired to a nearby fortress in the heart of the city, the Ciudadela, where he was besieged and bombarded by the Federal troops.

There now followed that sordid episode of Mexican history known as the Decena Trágica (the tragic ten days). Madero was full of fighting spirit, but Huerta, who now commanded the Federal troops in Mexico City, had decided to betray his master. While keeping up a desultory attack against the Ciudadela for the sake of appearances, he entered into secret negotiations with Felix Díaz. Meanwhile the United States ambassador was bringing heavy pressure upon Madero to resign. On 18 February, in a bloodless military coup, Madero and the vice-president were arrested in the national palace. On the same evening Huerta and Díaz met with Wilson in the US embassy, where it was agreed between the three men that Huerta would become provisional president, with Felix Díaz to succeed him just as soon as elections could be arranged. To make it look legal, the captive Madero was induced to resign so that, in accordance with the Constitution, the presidency devolved upon the foreign minister, Pedro Lascurain. The latter, in the only act of his one-day presidency, appointed Huerta to the Ministry of the Interior, and then himself resigned. By this trick Huerta became the legal president of Mexico. But there was worse to come. On 22 February Madero and Pino Suarez were taken out of the palace where they had been confined and driven to the back of the prison where they were shot in cold blood by their guards. The official explanation, which was accepted by both Huerta and Wilson, was that an attempt had been made to rescue the prisoners, and they had been accidentally shot in the affray.[2]

Huerta, a hard-drinking man who ruled the country from the bars which he frequented, was a typical example of the 'tough hombre' who so often crops up in Latin American history as the 'saviour' of his country in times of trouble. Rough diamond and alcoholic though he was, he made a good impression upon the elderly British Minister, Francis Stronge, and after a suitable pause for reflection the British government recognized the new Mexican government, not because it approved of Huerta morally, but because he seemed to be the only man in sight who was likely to be able to restore order, and thus safeguard the very considerable British investment in Mexico. The majority of Mexican and foreign business men took a similar view, and a number of professional men of irreproachable character were induced to join Huerta's cabinet.

But Woodrow Wilson, who became President of the USA in March 1913, was not prepared to follow the British lead. Without knowing very much about Mexican affairs, he was inclined to adopt a moralizing attitude. Huerta's and ambassador Wilson's part in the overthrow of Madero had come under heavy fire in the liberal press of North America. Responding to public pressure, the President decided to recall his namesake, who was subsequently dismissed ignominiously from the US diplomatic service. Withholding diplomatic recognition from Huerta, President Wilson sent his own personal emissary, John Lind, to Mexico with instructions to work for the peaceful retirement of Huerta, and the appointment of a more respectable provisional president whom the USA could recognize; after which, it was somewhat naïvely assumed in Washington, a free election would be held in Mexico with the consent of all parties. Needless to say, Lind, who did not speak a word of Spanish, did not get very far in his talks with the tough Mexican Dictator. Having eliminated all the supporters of Felix Díaz from his government and packed Congress with his own cronies, Huerta had no intention whatsoever of laying down his office at the bidding of the US President. In this stubborn attitude he received the tacit support of the new British Minister, Sir Lionel Carden, who had no use at all for the American policy and was convinced that it could only lead to disaster.

In retrospect, moral and ideological considerations apart, it seems doubtful whether it was sound thinking to suppose that a reactionary general like Huerta, however tough and able as a soldier, could hold the country down for very long. Zapata was still at large with his peasant army in Morelos. Madero, who had been unable to retain the support of his followers while he was alive, had become a martyr of the Revolution. Determined to avenge Madero's death, Pancho Villa raised a new force in Chihuahua and resumed his attacks upon the railways; Alvaro Obregón, who had already shown his mettle in earlier fighting, assumed command of a revolutionary army in Sonora; and in Coahuila a former governor of the State, Venustiano Carranza, a patriarchal figure with a flowing beard, took over-all charge of this northern revolt, announcing his 'Plan of Guadalupe', and assuming the title of First Chief of the Constitutionalist Army. Somewhat reluctantly Villa and Obregón acknowledged his leadership.

Huerta fought ferociously to try to break the circle of his enemies, but it was a hopeless task once President Wilson had decided to throw his weight behind Carranza and allow the latter's forces to be supplied with North American arms. The American president nearly wrecked his own policy, however, when he ordered the American fleet to occupy the port of Vera Cruz (27 April 1914) in an effort, so it was claimed, to prevent a cargo of munitions from reaching Huerta. Ignorant of Mexican psychology, Wilson was surprised and hurt when Carranza joined with Huerta in condemning this invasion of national sovereignty. But this American blunder came too late to save Huerta, who resigned on 27 April 1914 and departed into exile.

The constitutionalist cause had triumphed. But no sooner was victory won than the revolutionary leaders began to quarrel among themselves about the leadership, with Obregón supporting Carranza, and Villa and Zapata ganging up together in the opposition camp. At a convention of revolutionary generals and politicians held in Aguascalientes in October 1914, a supporter of Villa, Eulalio Gutiérrez, was nominated as provisional president. Carranza and Obregón retired to Vera Cruz where they set up a rival government.

And so the civil war continued. In December 1914 the two most colourful revolutionaries, Villa and Zapata, rode into Mexico City together; the citizens of the capital trembled as Villa's rough-riders hit up the night-spots and committed every kind of crime, while Zapata's white-clad peasants, although sporting ferocious-looking bandoliers and bristling with weapons, meekly rang the bells of rich men's houses to beg for something to eat. But by February 1915, after a long struggle during which the capital changed hands several times, Villa and Zapata were beaten in a series of battles (the one-armed Obregón turned out to be the best general of the Revolution) and Carranza was able to establish himself permanently in Mexico City. His government was recognized by the USA in the following October, and by the Spring of 1916 was in effective control of most of the country. Villa, now reduced to the status of a local *caudillo* and denied arms by the American government, retaliated by shooting sixteen unarmed American engineers in January 1916; two months later he crossed the border and raided the American city of Columbus, New Mexico, whereupon General Pershing[3] was ordered by Wilson to ride into Mexico with a posse of cavalry to capture 'the Mexican bandit' dead or alive. But Villa eluded his pursuers and lived on in the vastness of the northern desert until he was assassinated by political enemies in 1923. Zapata too fought on in the mountains of Morelos until in 1919 he was tricked into a meeting with a supposedly friendly general, ambushed and murdered. Both Villa and Zapata have become legends in Mexico. The latter, in particular, as the father of agrarian reform, is now firmly established in the pantheon of national heroes.

THE CONSTITUTION OF 1917

If Villa and Zapata, both men of the people, fit perfectly the popular image of the revolutionary guerrilla leader, Venustiano Carranza, who had emerged as the undisputed leader of the Mexican Revolution, looked more like a University president. A man of commanding presence and pontifical manner, he presided over his unruly crew of revolutionary supporters like a schoolmaster, obviously thoroughly enjoying his position of power, impatient of advice, and (according to his critics) liking the sound of his own voice. Although by background a landowner and a senator during the time of Díaz, Carranza could nevertheless claim good revolutionary credentials as one of the original supporters of Madero's revolution in 1911 and, after the latter's death, as the political leader of the opposition against Huerta. In this struggle he had to lean upon the support of President Wilson, but he was never a stooge of the Americans, always being quick to leap to the defence of Mexico's interests if the country's sovereignty or dignity was threatened by her powerful northern neighbour. An ardent nationalism, rather than reforming zeal, characterized his political outlook.

But although, like Madero, no more than a liberal (in the Juárez tradition) in his domestic politics, Carranza was a shrewd politician, very conscious of the wind of change now blowing through the country. His struggle for the leadership of the Revolution against Villa and Zapata had forced him to take up radical positions in public on such matters as agrarian and labour reform. Thus in 1915, while still in Vera Cruz, he became the sponsor of a bill for agrarian reform designed to steal the thunder from Zapata. Meanwhile, his right-hand man, Obregón, formed a close alliance with the labour leader, Luis Morones, at that time a leading light in the Casa Del Obrero Mundial, who organized six 'red battalions' of workers to fight for Carranza against the peasants and peons of Villa and Zapata. Thus *campesinos* and industrial workers found themselves temporarily on different sides in the Revolution, with the curious result that the basically conservative and middle-class Carranza acquired the reputation of being more of a radical than the proletarian and revolutionary Villa, whose cause increasingly attracted the support of the business community.

In 1916 Carranza summoned a convention (from which the supporters of Villa and Zapata were excluded) to draw up a new constitution. The draft which he submitted to the convention followed the traditional liberal lines and made only a few vague references to social reform. But although packed with his supporters, the convention, under the influence of a radical group led by General Francisco Múgica and supported by Obregón, produced in 1917 a document which was far more radical than Carranza had wanted. It was to become the basic charter of the Mexican Revolution. Unlike earlier liberal constitutions, which were concerned primarily with democratic guarantees of civil liberties, the Constitution of 1917 incorporated a wide range of social reforms.

To appease the demands of Zapata's militant peasants, Article 27 incorporated Carranza's agrarian law of 1915, providing for the restitution of lands to peasants who had been illegally dispossessed and a radical redistribution of landholdings in favour of semi-collective *ejidos* and small private farms. It did not abolish the *haciendas,* but the old-style feudal landowners were given clear notice that their day had ended.

To meet the clamour of the workers (both agrarian and industrial) for greater protection, Article 123 decreed that trade unions should become legal entities and be encouraged by the State; the right to strike was recognized; an eight-hour day was established with 'double time' paid for overtime; employers were made liable for accidents and occupational diseases; factories outside urban centres employing more than one hundred workers were obliged to maintain a dispensary and a school; mothers and children were protected by regulation from undue exploitation; a worker was to be paid three months' wages on dismissal; and so it went on. On paper at least this document turned Mexico into something like a workers' paradise.

To soothe the outraged feelings of nationalism which had been caused by Díaz's policy of allowing foreigners to become the owners of vast landed estates, and to exploit, with little benefit to Mexico, the country's precious resources in minerals and oil, it was decreed under Article 27 that the ownership of lands and waters, including the products of the sub-soil, were vested in the nation. These national properties could never be alienated, although the State had the right to transmit title thereto to private persons, thereby creating private property. Only Mexicans by birth or naturalization could own property, but the nation could grant the same right to foreigners provided that they agreed not to invoke the protection of their governments. Foreigners were forbidden to own land within a zone of 100 kilometres from frontiers or 50 kilometres from the sea coast. The State had the right to expropriate private property (whether foreign or Mexican) for reasons of public utility, but would indemnify the owners. By rejecting the liberal doctrine of the sanctity of private property, this important article reaffirmed the right of the State, which it had enjoyed in Spanish-colonial times, to regulate and limit property rights. In essence it was a declaration of national economic independence. By a stroke of the pen the privileged position of the powerful foreign farming, mining and oil interests was struck a deadly blow. It was not long before the cries of alarm and protest of these potentates were reverberating through the corridors of Washington and Whitehall.

For the rest, the new Constitution followed the well-trodden path of liberal democracy. It reaffirmed the principle of 'Effective Suffrage, No Re-election' to the presidency, and provided for universal male suffrage, a bi-cameral legislature, federalism, municipal liberty, division of powers, an independent judiciary, and the separation of Church from State. Primary education was to be free, compulsory and secular. Going even further than the anticlerical laws of Juárez, the Constitution included a series of draconian measures designed to curb the political power of the Roman Catholic Church – the Church could own no property, all religious buildings being the property of the State; monastic orders were forbidden; the priests had no vote, and could not hold public office or engage in political activities; the Church was debarred from owning or running its own primary schools; foreigners were forbidden to serve as priests; and the State legislatures were given the power to limit the number of priests who might officiate within their jurisdiction. To some extent, no doubt, these anticlerical measures were simply a hangover from the old liberal programme, but their greater severity reflected the feeling of the majority of the delegates that the Church was hostile to the Revolution, and therefore the State must be given the power to keep it firmly in its place.

Like all past documents of its kind, the Constitution of 1917 was a statement of aspirations rather than an immediate reality, but it did serve the practical purpose of charting a course for the Revolution. For the first time the aspirations of the peasants and workers, and the ideas of the intellectuals were fused into a comprehensive codification of social law. Unlike the liberal doctrines of the nineteenth century, which were very largely an importation from the USA, Britain and France, and therefore in many ways unsuited to Mexican conditions, the Constitution of 1917, anticipating by several years the Soviet Russian constitution, was essentially a statement of Mexican aspirations, arising out of Mexican conditions and experience.

THE SONORAN DYNASTY

Carranza, the unwilling father of this advanced constitution, was sufficiently a statesman to accept it without argument as representing the will of the people; but he was in no hurry to carry out its more radical provisions. His immediate preoccupations were to restore order after eight years of almost continuous fighting, and to put the finances of the country back on to a more or less even keel. He was energetic in asserting the national ownership of public lands and in resisting North American pressures; but he went slow on agrarian reform, distributing only 450,000 acres to 48,000 families during the whole period of his presidency. Nor did he prove to be a true friend of the labour unions which had supported his cause. The civil war had caused acute inflation, of which the workers were the most hard-hit victims. But when they organized a general strike, Carranza closed the Casa Del Obrero Mundial and arrested the strike leaders, including the powerful Luis Morones, who was condemned to death but later reprieved.

Thus when in 1920 the time came round for new elections, Carranza had lost his popularity with the revolutionary rank and file. The people turned instinctively towards Alvaro Obregón, the successful general from Sonora, as his obvious successor. But Carranza had other ideas. He had come to enjoy power, and while the constitution prevented him from standing himself for a second term, he sought to continue his rule indirectly by 'imposing' a friend as his successor, in the person of the politically unknown Ignacio Bonillas, the Mexican ambassador to Washington. This was too much for Obregón, who had been a good friend of Carranza in the past. In the last successful military revolt in Mexican history, Carranza was driven out of Mexico City, to lose his life ignominiously a little later while hiding in a bamboo hut in the mountains. The patriarchal statesman was murdered in cold blood on the orders of the general, Rudolfo Herrera, who was supposed to be assisting him in his flight. Thus yet another of Mexico's outstanding revolutionary leaders came to a bloody end. Adolfo de la Huerta, a fellow politician and friend of Obregón from Sonora, was named provisional president, pending the election of the latter later in the same year.

By background a small farmer from the north, Obregón was not only an excellent soldier, but he was a man of sound political judgement, with a sense of humour and a flair for making friends. At the beginning of his administration his chief support, apart from the army, came from the labour unions (CROM) organized since 1918 under the leadership of Luis Morones. But as a farmer, the new president, while by no means enthusiastic about agrarian reform, also had his ear open to the grievances of the peasants. He established agrarian commissions in each state to process the petitions of the villages, which had been ignored very largely during the time of Carranza. During Obregón's presidency some three million acres of land were distributed among 624 villages.

But perhaps the most notable achievement of Obregón's government was in the field of education. José Vasconcelos, a leading intellectual of the Revolution, was appointed Minister of Education; he threw all his tremendous energy into the task of building rural schools, which he regarded as the spearhead of the Revolution, in the belief that the village schoolmaster was destined to take over from the parish priest the task of educating the peasants in the new gospel of modern progress. This was the time, too, when the great Mexican muralists, Diego Rivera, Jose Clemente Orozco and David Siqueiros, began plastering the walls of Mexican public buildings with their mighty frescoes, telling the story of the Mexican Revolution in the crude red and black colours of the Marxist dialectic. This Marxist propaganda, combined with the tendency of Mexican politicians to overstress their revolutionary fervour in speeches made for domestic consumption, created considerable alarm in the USA. Fearing that Mexico had become a hotbed of bolshevism, Washington delayed recognition of Obregón's government for three years.

In fact Obregón was much more amenable than Carranza in his attitude towards foreign interests. As a gesture of appeasement he declared that Article 27 of the Constitution would not be applied retroactively, which meant that the mining and oil companies were secure in the possession of any properties acquired before 1917. But this did not satisfy the Americans, who were not prepared to accept Obregón's word and insisted on a formal treaty. Obregón angrily refused to comply; abandoning his policy of appeasement he imposed new taxes on the foreign oil companies which the latter regarded as confiscatory.

In 1924 Obregón was succeeded in the presidency by his principal lieutenant, General Plutarco Elías Calles, having first squashed a revolt by the other member of the Sonoran triumvirate, Adolfo de la Huerta. Calles had started life as a small-town schoolmaster and subsequently made his name as a revolutionary general. He was both more radical than Obregón in his political views – he described himself as a socialist – and more ruthless and dictatorial in his methods of government. Tough and dour, he lacked his predecessor's charm and bonhomie. But he pushed ahead vigorously with the revolutionary programme, stepping up the rate of land distribution, establishing a network of agricultural banks to supply credit to the *ejidos* and small farmers, promoting irrigation schemes on a national scale, carrying forward vigorously the education programme, building roads and encouraging the growth of local industry.

Nor was Calles afraid to enforce some of the more explosive articles of the Constitution of 1917 which Obregón had conveniently ignored. For example, the Roman Catholic Church, for obvious reasons, had always been openly hostile to the anticlerical provisions in that document, and was imprudent enough to make a public issue of the matter in a statement to the press in 1926. Calles retaliated by deporting two hundred alien priests and nuns, closing such Church-controlled primary schools as had survived, and ordering all the priests in the country to register with the civil authorities – all of which was in accordance with the rules that had been laid down in the Constitution, but had not until then been enforced. There was a storm of protest in conservative circles. The Mexican bishops, as unbending as Calles, ordered the priests not to register, and in protest against this requirement forbade them from officiating in the churches. For three long years no religious services of any kind were held in public in Mexico, although the churches remained open. In the cities members of the upper class invited priests to say mass in their private homes. In the traditionally Catholic states of Jalisco, Colima, and Michoacán the peasants revolted, burning government schools and attacking trains to the war cry of 'Cristo Rey' (Christ is King). The 'Cristero' rebellion was put down only after a great deal of bloodshed. Although the clergy disclaimed responsibility for this revolt, the government deported six of the bishops.

Calles also attempted to enforce the controversial Article 27 of the Constitution, which Obregón had agreed very largely to ignore, by decreeing that the owners of the oilfields should exchange their titles for fifty-year leases, dating from the time of acquisition. This provoked a storm of protest in the USA. The anger of the oil men, allied to the growing concern in that country about the 'religious persecution' (for that is how the exiled Mexican bishops in the USA described the anticlerical policy of the Calles government), brought relations between the two countries almost to the breaking point.

However, with the arrival in Mexico of a new US ambassador, Dwight Morrow, the threatening clouds were dissipated in an almost miraculous way. Morrow, although a banker by background, was a man of liberal outlook with a good deal of sympathy for what the Mexican Revolution was trying to achieve. Instead of attempting to browbeat or lecture Calles, he quickly won the heart of that iron man by travelling with him throughout the country in order to study its problems at first hand. At his suggestion, Calles agreed that the oil dispute should be submitted to the Mexican Supreme Court, which conveniently decided that the oil legislation was unconstitutional; it confirmed Obregón's ruling that foreigners who had acquired sub-soil rights before 1917 were entitled to full rights of ownership. Morrow also worked hard and to good effect to heal the quarrel with the Church. Thanks largely to his good offices, on 29 June 1929 the priests returned to the churches, and by the beginning of 1930 the last of the Cristero rebels had laid down their arms. But persecution of the Church continued in some of the states; for example in Tabasco where a fanatical governor, Garrido Cannabal, decreed that no priest could enter the state unless he were legally married – a monstrous ruling which effectively put a stop to all religious activities in that tropical backwater.[4]

Calles completed his presidency in 1928, having first amended the Constitution in order to allow Obregón to succeed him for a second term. Both men, in spite of their revolutionary background, believed in strong government, with virtually all the power concentrated in the hands of the president. They had come to the conclusion that the best way of continuing and consolidating the gains of the Revolution, and of keeping the unruly revolutionary family in order, was to create an unofficial dynasty based on the understanding that the two Sonoran generals would alternate in office at regular four-year intervals. After putting down two abortive military revolts – for this doctrine was very far from being popular in revolutionary circles – Obregón was duly re-elected to the presidency as had been planned. But three weeks later he was assassinated by a young religious fanatic. It does not seem to have been a political crime.

Calles now stood alone. The Constitution prohibited his immediate re-election to the presidency, but he continued to rule behind the scenes with the unofficial title of 'Supreme Chief of the Revolution' during the short presidencies of Emilio Portes Gil (1928–30), Pascual Ortiz Rubio (1930–32) and General Abelardo Rodríguez (1932–34). In 1928 the National Revolutionary Party (PNR) was established by Calles and Portes Gil in order to co-ordinate all the political groups – labour, agrarian and middle class – from which the revolutionary movement drew its support. With various successive changes in its organization and title this revolutionary party, under a series of strong presidents, has ruled the country ever since.

Portes Gil, a radical lawyer and former governor of Tamaulipas, pushed forward energetically with the programme of the Revolution during his short term as provisional president, distributing land at a faster rate than any of his predecessors, and freeing the labour movement from the growing tyranny of the CROM, whose leaders had grown rich with the spoils of office and no longer cared about the problems of the working class. But there was a noticeable slackening in the tempo of revolutionary change under his successors. Pascual Ortiz Rubio, nicknamed contemptuously Pascualito by the people, was completely dominated by Calles; when he began to show some signs of independence he was ignominiously bundled out of office by the strong man. The next president, General Abelardo Rodríguez, whom Calles now chose to preside over the destinies of the nation, was a member of a small group of privileged supporters who had made fortunes out of the Revolution, and flaunted their wealth in ostentatious villas in Cuernavaca. A wealthy man, Rodríguez – the owner of two flourishing casinos among his many interests – spoke the jargon of the Revolution in which he had been brought up, but was essentially a businessman's president. Calles himself, during this last phase of his influence, had become increasingly conservative in his political ideas. Perhaps under the influence of Morrow, who took a businessman's view of Mexico's problems, Calles became disillusioned with the poor economic results of the agrarian programme, and virtually put a stop to the distribution of land. The one-time socialist now saw the future of the country in terms of industrial development which, in alliance with local and foreign capital, he did his best to foster.

Calles is a controversial figure. While his economic policies and strong-man rule were welcomed with relief by the businessmen, he was bitterly hated in his time by the majority of Mexican conservatives because of his persecution of the Church. By the left wing politicians he was condemned as a man who had started well but ended by betraying the Mexican Revolution. There is a tendency, however, among modern historians to assess the achievements of Calles in a very much more favourable light. Having failed to establish a personal dynasty in alliance with Obregón, he had the good sense to build, through the creation of the PNR, a political framework which has served the country well ever since, providing more or less democratic machinery for the selection of presidential candidates, while ensuring that during his tenure of office the President of Mexico will enjoy the fullest possible executive power. Thus, if Mexico has enjoyed remarkable political stability during the last forty years, she owes it very largely to Calles. Nor in retrospect does it seem fair to condemn Calles for betraying the Revolution. What he did was to recognize the hard fact that social, and above all agrarian reform would be of little value to the recipients unless based on solid economic foundations. He was the first of the revolutionary presidents to grasp the urgent need for pushing forward with the expansion of the economy's infrastructure, and to begin preparing the ground for the tremendous growth which has taken place in Mexico during the last thirty years.

THE CLIMAX

When General Lazaro Cárdenas (1934-40) succeeded to the presidency, it was generally assumed in Mexico that Calles would continue to rule the country from behind the scenes. As a revolutionary general, and later as governor of Michoacán, Cárdenas had acquired the reputation of being something of a radical; indeed Calles had endorsed his candidature precisely for this reason, in order to appease the restive and suspicious left wing of the PNR. But Cárdenas, unlike some of his more cynical colleagues in the PNR, not only 'talked Revolution', but sincerely believed that the survival of the revolutionary movement depended on keeping faith with the masses. As he stumped the country, visiting the most remote villages, it became uncomfortably clear to the now conservative Calles that the presidential candidate really believed in the six-year plan which the party intellectuals had concocted to serve as the basis of the electoral campaign. Regarded by Calles as window-dressing, in the eyes of Cárdenas this document was no mere scrap of paper to be thrown away once office had been achieved, but a serious programme for action and reform to which his government would be pledged to devote all its energies.

A sincere democrat, and at the same time a shrewd politician, Cárdenas set the tone for his administration by refusing to live in Chapultepec castle, the traditional residence of viceroys and presidents, and moving to more modest quarters at Los Pinos. In a further democratic gesture he closed down the casinos (two of them the property of ex-President Rodríguez) which had been a favourite haunt of nouveau-riche revolutionaries during the previous regime. Then, with the acclaim of the multitude ringing in his ears, he got down to the serious business of the six-year plan. Reversing the go-slow policy of Calles, the new president drastically stepped up the pace of land distribution, and he was unstinting in his support of the labour unions. When the businessmen in Monterrey complained about the wave of strikes which ensued, Cárdenas told them in so many words that either they must learn to live with the Revolution or get out.

All this was too much for Calles. On 12 June 1935, the Supreme Chief, in one of his rare public utterances, reaffirmed his faith in conservative solutions of the country's problems, reminding the people slyly of the fate of President Ortiz Rubio, who had been forced out of office when he tried to pursue an independent policy. 'Viva Calles' was the heartfelt cry of the business community. But Cárdenas was not the man to lie down under such a threat. In open defiance of the Supreme Chief he purged his cabinet of all the friends and supporters of Calles. On 19 June 1935, to the great surprise of everybody, it was Calles, not Cárdenas, who found it prudent to leave the capital, as a first step along the road to retirement. In the following year, when he tried once more to interfere, Calles was banished to the USA.

Now the undisputed master of Mexico, Cárdenas further consolidated his position by eliminating all leading Callistas from the army, state-governorships and the PNR. He reorganized the Revolutionary Party on functional lines and renamed it Partido de la Revolucion Mexicana (PRM). The new party consisted of four sectors – labour, agrarian, popular and military. The unions comprising the labour sector were organized in a new Federation (CTM) founded in 1936, of which the Communist, Lombardo Toledano, became the Secretary

General, replacing as labour boss the discredited leader of the CROM, Luis Morones, who departed with Calles into exile abroad. The agrarian sector was composed of peasant leagues organized in the Confederation Nacional Campesina (CNC) and based on the collective *ejidos*, which Cárdenas favoured in preference to the small private farms upon which, in their agrarian policies, Obregón and Calles had pinned their hopes. The so-called 'popular' sector was created to represent the interests of the white-collar middle class, and included such important organizations as those of the civil servants and the schoolteachers. The military sector, which has since been eliminated from the party machinery, represented the political interests of the army leaders. Although no longer active in politics (this had been one of the great achievements of Calles) the army nevertheless underpinned the whole political structure. No longer the revolutionary rabble of early days, it was now a well organized professional force upon whose loyalty the stability of the regime ultimately depended.

Assured of popular support through this improved party machinery, but keeping the reins of power firmly in his hands in accordance with the now well established custom of Mexican Presidents, Cárdenas went further than any of his predecessors along the path of revolutionary change which had been charted by the authors of the Constitution of 1917. Under his determined onslaught the three already tottering pillars of the Porfirian establishment – the feudal landowners, the Roman Catholic Church and the foreign capitalists – collapsed, being replaced by a new order of society, which, even if it was not completely democratic, was certainly much more broadly based than anything that had existed in Mexico before.

During his six years in office Cárdenas distributed twice as much land as had been given to the peasants by all the previous revolutionary governments put together. Most politicians until that time had regarded the *ejido* as a device for assuaging the land hunger of militant peasants, realizing that the distribution of hacienda lands to untutored peasants would inevitably result in a loss of production. This is indeed why Calles had lost faith in the agrarian programme and brought it virtually to a stop. But Cárdenas was a passionate believer in the virtues of the collective *ejido*. He thought that they could be made economically viable if properly managed on co-operative lines, with the assistance of the government, and turned to the production of commercial crops. Towards this end he accelerated irrigation, established agricultural schools and initiated rural community projects. His most ambitious scheme for co-operative farming was in the Laguna district, near Torreón, where thirty-eight thousand peasant families were settled on rich irrigated cotton land taken from the *haciendas*, and elaborate arrangements made through the new National Ejidal Bank to finance this co-operative venture and provide technical advice and supervision.

In his relations with the Roman Catholic Church Cárdenas began by adopting a strict policy of enforcing the anticlerical provisions of the Constitution, in particular with regard to education. But he became more lenient in his attitude towards the Church once he had consolidated his position and no longer had to compete with Calles. In 1935 the unpopular 'socialist' education (the invention of a left-wing near-communist, Minister of Education, Narciso Bassols) was replaced by less dogmatic, but 'patriotic' teaching in the public schools, designed, not to turn the children into little Marxists, but to make them take a pride in their country and the achievements of the Revolution. Thus Cárdenas, while firmly upholding the primacy of the State in education, took the heat out of the religious controversy and inaugurated a period of peaceful co-existence between Church and State which has lasted to this day.

Without doubt the most notable aspect of the policy of Cárdenas was the tough nationalistic line he took when dealing with foreign capital. He was not, he used to claim, opposed to foreign capital as such, but he insisted that foreign investors in Mexico must be prepared to abide by Mexican rules. He was not prepared to tolerate any longer a situation in which the major foreign companies habitually appealed to their own governments for protection, in this way exerting 'imperialistic' pressures on the Mexican government. In his first major coup directed against foreign capital Cárdenas took over control of the railways. This was not, however, so dramatic a step as it might seem. Most of the railways already belonged to the Mexican government. But the foreign bondholders, who had financed their construction, were still in a position to exercise a powerful influence over their management. Cárdenas removed this source of irritation by the simple device of incorporating the railway debt into the general foreign debt, leaving the Mexican government free to manage the railways as it saw fit.

Going to more spectacular lengths, on 18 March 1938, Cárdenas decreed the expropriation of the entire oil industry. As we saw, American and British oil companies had come to Mexico in good faith, and with the encouragement of Díaz, to open up and exploit her vast potentialities of oil, and they had done a good job from a technical point of view. But they had become extremely unpopular in revolutionary circles by the time of Cárdenas. Most of the oil, and all the profits from the industry, went abroad; very little was left behind in Mexico beyond the product of such taxes as could be collected, royalties on land, and the wages – good ones by Mexican standards – which were paid to the Mexican workers in the oilfields and refineries. But the latter for the most part performed only the most menial functions; all the best jobs in the industry were reserved for an aristocracy of foreign managers and technicians, who lived in comparative luxury in their well-appointed encampments, while the workers were housed in makeshift shanty-towns. But the worst crime of the oil companies, in Mexican eyes, was their reluctance to comply with the terms of the Constitution of 1917, in regard to such matters as concessions and sub-soil rights, and the powerful diplomatic support they had sought and obtained from successive American governments. It was above all the 'imperialistic machinations' of the oil potentates (whether real or suspected) which had caused resentment and hardened the determination of the officials who surrounded Cárdenas to put the oil companies in their place.

A massive pay demand was the instrument utilized by the Mexican government in order to bring the companies to heel. A Mexican board of arbitration, after hearing evidence from the unions and the companies, ordered the latter to pay wage increases totalling twenty-six million pesos, and to give their workers certain rights of participation in management. The companies were opposed to the latter and in regard to the former vigorously disputed the accuracy of the Mexican figures (they estimated the real cost of the award at forty-one million pesos as against claimed profits of only twenty-three million pesos) and appealed to the Mexican Supreme Court. But the latter body (which was packed with the supporters of Cárdenas) upheld the verdict of the arbitration board. When the companies still refused to accept the award as it stood, Cárdenas lost all patience and, condemning their 'rebellious' attitude, ordered their properties to be seized.[5]

The historic action of Cárdenas in daring to do battle with the oil giants was hailed with enthusiasm by the vast majority of Mexicans. It caused a surge of pride and jubilation such as Mexico had never experienced before, and this overrode any doubts that may have existed in the more cautious minds about Mexico's ability to run the oil industry (the companies were convinced that it could not), or cope with the major international crisis which this action had provoked. It is difficult at this distance of time to remember, or understand, the anger which swept through the City of London and Wall Street as 'Mexican Eagles' and other popular oil stocks plummeted into the depths. Today it would be difficult to find a British or North American commentator on Mexican affairs who did not take for granted the justice of Cárdenas's bold action. But, as I well remember – I sent the first story of the expropriation to the London *Times* – this was not at all the way in which the matter was judged at the time in the great financial centres of the world. With the almost sole exception of Mr Kingsley Martin in the *New Statesman*, the British press was solid in its condemnation of Mexico. The phrase coined by Evelyn Waugh for the title of his angry book about Mexico, 'Robbery under Law', summed up very well the outraged feelings of the City.

Even so, Cárdenas was batting on a good international wicket. Britain delivered a series of such sharp notes as to cause Mexico to break off diplomatic relations with her. But the USA, under the guidance of President Franklin Roosevelt, took a much more moderate line, recognizing the right of the Mexican Government to expropriate the properties of US citizens in Mexico, provided that adequate compensation were paid. In part this moderation was a reflection of the Good Neighbour Policy which had replaced 'dollar diplomacy' as the guiding light for US policy. Even more, no doubt, it reflected Roosevelt's concern with the gathering war clouds in Europe. As seen in Washington, it was essential for strategic reasons that the USA should remain on friendly terms with Mexico. Whatever may have been its faults, the 'democratic' government of Cárdenas was regarded by US officials as the safest bet from an ideological point of view in a Latin America torn between the rival claims of communism and fascism. The latter creed in a diluted form, encouraged by General Franco's victory in the Spanish civil war, had acquired some following in Mexico among people who were tired of the Revolution and disapproved of Cárdenas's social policies.

A right-wing coup d'état in Mexico, such as General Saturnino Cedillo attempted to launch from San Luis Potosí shortly after the expropriation, would have been a decided setback for the hard-pressed democratic cause on the eve of World War 2. Nor, when the international oil companies tried to impose a boycott on Mexican oil, can the State Department have been at all happy to see the Germans and the Japanese stepping into the breach, with offers to purchase Mexican oil under barter arrangements. In such a dangerous inter-national situation the obvious policy for the USA was to be gentle with Cárdenas and not make too much of a fuss about a little spilt oil.

Assured of benevolent US support, Cárdenas, having quickly and easily crushed the rebellion of Cedillo, was able to end his presidency in triumph. As the author of the oil expropriation his name will always have an honoured place in Mexican history, although there are many Mexicans today within the Revolutionary fold who disapprove of his radicalism. But on the oil question he stands above criticism. After some growing pains Pemex, the Mexican Govern-ment's oil corporation, has become a flourishing concern, not only producing vast quantities of oil and gas (mainly used now for internal consumption), but it is also in the process of developing an impressive petro-chemical industry. The compensation which some years later it was agreed amicably to pay to the dispossessed British and American oil companies has been paid in full and on the nail. Meanwhile, an ironical touch, Pemex is now Britain's best customer in Mexico.

In retrospect, the six years of the presidency of Cárdenas can be seen as the climax of the thirty-year-old Mexican Revolution. The convulsion had cost the country more than a million lives, and caused untold damage to property. It had almost certainly retarded the natural growth of the economy during those troubled years. But more important than any temporary damage it may have caused, the Revolution had succeeded at last in breaking down the barriers of a caste-ridden feudal society. Most important of all perhaps, it had given the Mexican people a new sense of national pride and identity.

POSTSCRIPT

Cárdenas was succeeded in the presidency in December 1946 by General Avila Camacho. The PNR had had to chose between the rival claims of General Francisco J. Mugica, the left-wing author of the 1917 Constitution and the logical successor of Cárdenas, and a more moderate candidate. The majority of the party elders, with the agreement of Cárdenas, opted for a period of stability. It was felt that a slowing down of the revolutionary pace was needed in order to consolidate the advances made by Cárdenas and safeguard the economy which, already under great strain, was now threatened with disruption by the onset of World War 2. As it was, Camacho had to fight hard in the election to defeat the independent right-wing candidate, General Juan Andreu Almazán, who was campaigning against the PNR on the slogan that Cárdenas and his supporters were communists. Thanks to the control of the PNR over the voting machinery, Camacho won the election with an impressive majority, but there are some observers who think that this result did not reflect the true feelings of the electorate.

Be this as it may, Camacho, a believing Roman Catholic, a champion of small property ownership in the countryside, a soldier of fundamentally conservative political outlook, was just the man to give the country the rest it needed. While continuing to profess allegiance to the basic principles of the Revolution (the PNR continued as the dominant factor in politics), he inaugurated the period of 'consolidation' which under a series of able presidents has continued to the present day. According to the official party line, the Revolution still went on; it was only the problems of the country which had changed with the passing of the years. The old order had been finally destroyed by Cárdenas. Now the most pressing need was economic development, without which, it was thought, there could be no real further advance on the social front.

Thus, as Calles had done before him, Camacho devoted most of his energies to economic and industrial development. In this endeavour he was greatly helped by the demand for manufactured goods created by the second World War. Camacho, sincerely believing in the democratic cause, and with a shrewd eye to the main chance, brought Mexico into the war on the side of the Allies, working in close co-operation with the USA on the economic front to the great and lasting benefit of Mexico's economy. As a result of his policies the gross national product doubled during his presidency.

Camacho's successor. Miguel Alemán (1946–52), pushed forward with the programme of industrialization and economic development with even greater vigour. Under his youthful and dynamic leadership, everything was sacrificed for the sake of rapid capital accumulation both domestically (a new class of Mexican entrepreneurs came into being) and by encouraging foreign capital to return to Mexico under suitable national safeguards. In terms of material development – roads, dams, irrigation, ports, airfields, schools, hospitals, mining expanded, agriculture diversified and oriented towards export markets and, above all, new industries created – the results of the policy were impressive. But these economic advances were secured at a heavy price in social terms. Wages were kept down, while inflation caused prices to rise. The emphasis of agricultural policy was shifted from the redistribution of land among needy peasants (the most cherished ideal of the Revolution) to more efficient production. While the people tightened their belts, the favoured politicians and businessmen who surrounded Alemán made fortunes – a repetition in a more sophisticated form of the phenomenon of 'revolutionary millionaires' that had characterized the latter days of the Calles dictatorship.

Alemán represented the spirit of the new generation of Mexicans who had not lived through the Revolution, and for whom the old party slogans were no longer meaningful except in a purely symbolic and traditional sense like Magna Carta to the British, or the Declaration of Independence to the Americans. A conservative in politics (he vigorously purged the trade unions of communist elements), Alemán was progressive in his economic policies, believing in the virtues of a mixed economy, in which vast state enterprises co-existed with private firms, and with the motive power furnished by a balanced mixture of private initiative and state planning. The idol of many Mexicans in the official party and outside who shared his views, Alemán was unpopular both with the more conservative members of the business community, who believed in untrammelled free enterprise, and the old-guard rank and file of the Revolutionary Party who considered that he had sacrificed the interests of the peasants and the working class on the altar of Mammon.

These proletarian feelings of resentment came to a head when the party managers (the Party had been rechristened Partido Revolucionario Institucional) were faced with the problem of choosing a successor to Alemán. The left wing, under the leadership of Cárdenas, clamorously demanded more progressive social policies – a better deal for the man on the farm or in the street. Responding to this popular pressure, Alemán's successors, Adolfo Ruiz Cortines (1952–58), Adolfo López Mateos (1958–64) and Gustavo Díaz Ordaz (1964–70) have paid more regard to the interests of the peasants and the workers, with a return to an active policy of agrarian reform and the development of social services, while continuing vigorously with the programme of industrialization. Their aim has been to achieve balanced growth between industry and agriculture, and to harmonize the demands of economic development with social justice. Thus, while Cárdenas, who until his death in 1970 exerted great influence behind the scenes as the Grand Old Man of the Revolution, represents its social conscience, and Alemán is the prophet of economic progress, the modern trend in Mexican leadership is to seek a middle road between these two extremes.

It will be clear from the foregoing summary that a profound change in the revolutionary image has taken place during the last thirty years. Gone from the political scene are picturesque guerrilla leaders like Pancho Villa or Emiliano Zapata. The modern generation of political leaders were small children or still unborn when Madero raised the standard of revolt in 1910. Modern Mexican presidents (since Alemán they have all been civilians) are essentially technocrats; they are more like the president of some huge business corporation than the leader of a revolution. But even though left wing critics may complain that the Mexican Revolution really came to an end with Cárdenas (and is it indeed possible for a revolution to become an institution?) the progress of Mexico during the last thirty years has been truly remarkable, whether one calls it a revolution or not.

18 Part of the Quintana Roo territory, from the air. With its huge areas of unending jungle, this is real Graham Greene country.

19 Mexico City: the magnificent, tree-lined Paseo de la Reforma, dominated by skyscraper office blocks and hotels.

20, 21 The traditional and the modern live side by side in Mexico. *Above:* Tarascan Indians casting their butterfly nets for fish in Lake Pátzcuaro. *Left:* native pottery in a Mexico City market stall.

22 *Opposite:* Part of the great refinery and petro-chemical plant of the state-owned Pemex at Minatitlán.

23 Laying irrigation pipes to serve the agricultural areas of Jalisco.

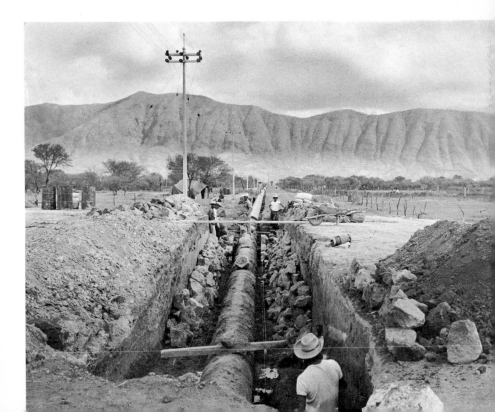

24 Mexican architecture is not afraid of bold and striking innovations. The Tlatelolco tower (*above*) is the focal point of a vast new building development in Mexico City.

25 The University Library in Mexico City, beautifully decorated with a mural by Diego Rivera.

26 The Square of the Three Cultures in Mexico City shows at a glance the three stages of Mexico's evolution – its ancient Indian past, the Spanish colony, and the multi-storied pinnacles of the modern state.

27 Luis Echeverría at a presidential election meeting in 1970. As
the official candidate of the National Revolutionary Party (PRI) he was
elected with 84 per cent of the total vote.

28, 29 *Opposite, above:* Enriqueta Basilio carries the Olympic torch
during the opening ceremonies for the Olympic Games in 1968 – the
first woman to perform this rite. The games were marred by the student
demonstrations which took place on 2 October 1968 and resulted in
a bloody clash between the demonstrators and the army. Two hundred
people were killed and a number of students arrested (*opposite below*).

30 In spite of its rapid modernization and industrial development, Mexico still observes the traditional fiestas. During the Vanilla Festival at Papantla, Vera Cruz, descendants of the Totonacs of 1500 years ago enact the Rain Dance ceremonies, of which this human ferris wheel is a part. The headdress is dazzling, with mirrors and coloured beads.

8   Society in transition

AT THE TURN OF THE CENTURY Mexico was still a rural and feudal society, with a handful of leading white families monopolizing virtually all the wealth, while some eighty per cent of the population, Indians and mestizos, laboured as peasants in the fields under conditions of feudal serfdom, or sweated it out in the mines and the few ill-equipped factories which then existed. A middle class, such as we know it in Europe or the United States of America, hardly existed; such as it was, it accounted for less than ten per cent of the population.

Today, seventy years later, half of the population of Mexico live in the cities; an estimated forty per cent[1] of Mexicans live in reasonable comfort and can claim to have achieved middle class or a higher status in society. Thus modern Mexico contains two entirely different worlds. In the countryside a diminishing but still uncomfortably large residue of extremely poor Indian and mestizo peasants continue to live in the old traditional way, tilling pathetically small plots of land, and producing only enough to keep their families alive. In contrast the cities belong to the affluent society of the modern world. Urban wages on average are much higher than in the countryside. Out of every hundred homes in Mexico City 97 have wireless sets and 82 have television. One out of every four families owns a motor car.[2] For the Mexican peasant these luxuries represent opulence beyond his wildest dreams. Thus in Mexico the middle class may be said to begin with the relatively well-paid unionized workers in industry, whose standard of life, both in terms of wages and social amenities, is incomparably better than that of the peasants and those unskilled workers who have not yet found their feet in an urban environment. It progresses upwards on a rising scale of affluence and social prestige through the white-collar and professional classes, until it merges with the rich managerial and technocratic upper class, which at the summit of the social pyramid has replaced the old landed oligarchy.

But there is also in Mexico a third, transitional world – a world of mingled hope and despair – lying along the border which separates the primitive order of the countryside from the modern life of the cities. As the new highways push their way relentlessly into the most remote corners of the country, so once primitive communities become increasingly subjected to urban influences and their character changes. The village elders cling tenaciously to the old ways, but the young become restless; many peasant families have migrated to the cities in search of a better life. But there are more immigrants than jobs, with the result that today all the larger Mexican cities are ringed with shanty-towns in which the sons and the daughters of the peasants live in squalor and misery, belonging neither to the town nor to the country, and desperate for work of any kind.

Thus in modern Mexico there is to be found every kind of social condition ranging from the direst poverty to ostentatious opulence. The rich man's Cadillac competes for living space on the streets with the mestizo vendor's heavily laden handcart; under the shadow of great skyscrapers people live in hovels; a poor Indian woman, with her baby carried in a shawl on her back, sells matches outside the bursting supermarket; in the parks and gardens grubby little boys offer shoe-shines to well-heeled citizens. Visitors to Mexico are often shocked by these glaring contrasts between riches and poverty. But before passing hasty judgement, they should pause to reflect upon the magnitude of the problems which have faced the leaders of the Mexican Revolution: a colonial legacy of racial and class prejudices and rigidities; the poverty, ignorance and apathy of the peasants; the harsh character of the environment; the lack until very recently of a modern infrastructure; an industrial revolution which in 1910 was still in its infancy; the ravages of prolonged civil war; economic growth running a desperate race against a population explosion. Faced with such formidable difficulties it is surely a miracle that the Mexicans have achieved so much in so little time.

The Revolution has destroyed the rigid class structure of colonial and Porfirian days, engendering in its place a high rate of social mobility; so that, in theory at any rate, there are no longer any racial or social barriers to prevent a man from improving his situation in society. Many people are doing just this, with the beneficial result, as we saw, that Mexico now has a comparatively large and prosperous middle class. Illiteracy has been cut down from eighty per cent to less than a quarter of the population. While there is still a wide gulf between rich and poor, the wealth of the country is much more widely spread than it was sixty years ago. The economy has been transformed and modernized out of all recognition, to the benefit, if not of all, at least of a substantial proportion of the Mexican people.

Not that the Mexicans are complacent about their achievements. 'The Revolution is not yet over', declared Luis Echeverría, in his inaugural speech, on 15 November 1969, as the presidential candidate of the PRI. 'Its challenge – its principal task – is to reduce the gap between the powerful and the weak, and prevent the wealth of Mexico, created by the work of the people, from becoming concentrated in a few hands'. This being his professed creed, let us examine some of the problems which lie in wait for the new president.

THE AGRARIAN PROBLEM

When the Revolution began to develop a philosophy the agrarian problem was conceived primarily in terms of social justice. Land that had been stolen from the peasants by the great landowners must be returned to its rightful owners; regardless of legal rights, landless peasants must be given a plot of land for the use of their families; the suffocating power of the owners of the great *haciendas* must be broken and the peasants freed from the shackles of feudal serfdom. But there was never an agreed policy among the Revolutionary leaders about what should be the pattern of land tenure once the great *haciendas* had disappeared. The purists in the agrarian movement, headed by Cárdenas, wanted to rebuild the rural economy on the basis of the collective village *ejidos*, an institution which had its roots in Aztec times. It was a romantic idea which fitted in well with the tendency to give the Revolution an Indian ideology, and it was what most of the peasants themselves wanted. But Obregón, Calles and indeed most of the later revolutionary leaders, while forced to pay lip-service to the merits of the *ejido*, thought that the future for Mexican agriculture lay rather with the small independent farmer in outright possession of his own land. Although it was much criticized at the time, some modern investigators[3] claim that the experiment of collective farming made by Cárdenas in the Laguna area had considerable success; the peasants under competent direction, worked

131

efficiently and reaped substantial profits. However, after 1940, under the more conservative government of Avila Camacho, funds for the scheme, which was socialist in its implications, were drastically cut. Alemán, with his bias towards capitalistic solutions of the nation's problems, amended the agrarian laws so as to permit larger individual holdings of land for the efficient production of export crops, and to encourage large-scale ranching. Both he and his successors initiated major irrigation and land reclamation schemes in the arid north and in the tropical regions of the south to provide more land for agriculture.

The battle still rages within the ranks of the PRI, with the political representatives of the *ejidos* fighting a tenacious rearguard action against the supporters of the independent landowner and the concept of large scale farming run on capitalistic lines. In spite of these differences in approach the progress of agrarian reform in Mexico is impressive. Before the Revolution one per cent of the population owned virtually all the land. But in the forty years between 1910 and 1950 the number of farms in Mexico rose from 48,000 to 1.4 million, a remarkable testimony to the thoroughness of the redistribution of land which has been carried out by successive Revolutionary governments. It is estimated that today some 40 per cent of the land cultivable in Mexico belongs to the *ejidos*; these communal lands are divided up for the most part in small lots among the peasants for their individual use, but cannot be sold or mortgaged. The rest of the land is owned outright by the individual farmers, about half of it again in very small lots worked by peasant families, the rest in larger holdings owned for the most part by proprietors living in the cities who regard their farms as a business investment.[4] Thus to a very large extent the *latifundio* (over-large estate) has been replaced by the *minifundio* of only a few acres which is not economically viable; the *latifundio* still exists in some areas (the owners get round the law by dividing their properties among members of their family and pooling their resources). These large estates have the scale and capitalization to afford modern techniques, mechanization and good management. About five per cent of the rural labour force, working on these more efficient farms, produces about half the national agricultural product. Two-thirds of the rural population, cultivating their mini-plots, live at subsistence level on the margin of the money economy.

Faced with such grim statistics, one can understand the growing doubts of Calles about the virtues of indiscriminate land redistribution; indeed since the time of the presidency of Cárdenas agrarian policy, while continuing to promote land redistribution as a political necessity, has concentrated more and more upon efforts to increase agricultural productivity by such means as irrigation, land reclamation and the provision to farmers of credit, seeds, fertilizers and insecticides. During the last twenty-five years no less than ten per cent of the federal budget has been spent on irrigation, with the almost miraculous result that the bone-dry states of Sinaloa, Sonora and Lower California now account for one quarter of the agricultural income of the country. In regions which were formerly completely desert a series of rich man-made oases grow commercial crops such as cotton, wheat, sugar and tomatoes. Similarly, in the tropical lowlands, thanks to such vast reclamation schemes as those in the Balsas and Papaloapan valleys, rice and sugar cane now grow where once there was only jungle, or at best a few scattered plantations of bananas. The same thing happened on the slopes of the Sierra Madre, leading up into the temperate zone where coffee plantations and citrus orchards have been created out of the wilderness. Higher up on the plateau, on the better land, the traditional maize has been replaced by wheat and the cultivation of vegetables and fruit. Thanks to these various efforts Mexico's cultivated area has been increased by more than 40 per cent since 1939, production has trebled during the last twenty-five years, and productivity has risen – for example, the yield on Mexican wheat, although still very low by US standards, has doubled since 1950. Mexico is today virtually self-sufficient in home-grown food and produces surpluses for export in most of the principal crops. But there still remains the problem of the mini-farmer.

In a speech formally accepting his nomination for the presidency, Echeverría declared that 'the roots of Mexico are in the soil and that is where we must return to give our progress new impulse'. Promising to make the welfare of Mexico's impoverished subsistence farmers the main concern of his administration, the candidate spoke of the need to implement 'the second stage' of agrarian reform by employing capital and technology to raise the productivity of land already distributed – the 'first stage', namely that of land redistribution, which began over fifty years ago, being virtually completed. For of the 74 million acres of potentially cultivable land in Mexico, all except some very marginal areas have been put in production and are already in the hands of the farmers. Since only limited opportunities remain to increase Mexico's cultivated acreage, any future gains in agricultural output will have to come mainly from more intensive use of existing lands and greater crop yields. But the difficulties are formidable. Modern mechanized farming can only be practised on the flatlands – a rare geographical condition in Mexico. Most of Mexico's small farmers hoe small uneconomic plots of maize and beans on unirrigated mountain slopes on which a tractor and plough could not be used.

The remedy can only lie in the promotion of local schemes for irrigation and other such improvements to the land, livestock developments, and the provision of credit and technical assistance for the small farmer. In the wider context the need is for education (both general and technical) and the opening up of communications in order to bring the Indian peasants living in the more remote areas into touch with the modern world. Towards these ends an Indigenous Institute was founded in 1949 under the direction of Dr Alfonso Caso, Mexico's leading archeologist and anthropologist. This body does excellent work in backward parts of the country, for example in Chiapas, supplying clinics and schools, training doctors, nurses and teachers, building roads, improving water supplies, providing electricity, encouraging local trade, and introducing new methods of agriculture. The peasants have shown themselves to be apt pupils. It is a delicate task, however. Bright young Indian pupils are apt to take to bourgeois ways and despise their own origins. There is a danger too that the traditional code of ethics, characterized by such old-fashioned virtues as dignity, serenity, prudence, honesty, courtesy and hard work, will be replaced by less desirable qualities – a disdain of parents and the village elders, resentment, class consciousness and restlessness, with the young people tending to drift away from the village, where their better education could have been useful, probably to end up in the city slums.[5]

In rural communities nearer to the centre of things no artificial stimulus by the government is needed to bring them closer to the modern world – it is happening in any case – although here again the results of the changes may not be all to the good. The village of Tepoztlán, which nestles beneath the cliffs of a mountain range in Morelos, is a good example of such an evolving rural community;

it has been the subject of three separate anthropological surveys, the first carried out by Robert Redfield in 1926–27, the last two by Oscar Lewis, who restudied the village in 1951 and then returned, to see what changes had taken place, for a second period in 1956–57.[6] Tepoztlán is a typical Mexican village, although somewhat larger than normal, with an old and stable population whose roots lie deeply buried in the colonial and Indian past. The basic economic activity is agriculture, with the primitive hoe used to cultivate the plots on the mountain slopes; oxen and the plough being employed on the flat land of the valley bottom. The crops are the traditional maize, beans and squash and produce no more than a bare living for the farmers. Local industry in the village is still very primitive. Barter persists in the market, although the people also participate in a money economy. Many pre-hispanic traits have persisted – a system of communal land ownership and social organization which goes back in time for four hundred years or more; material survivals such as adobe walls, clay-plastered granaries for the maize, the three-legged grinding stone, the clay griddle, the mortar and pestle, the native sandal or *huarache*; and, in food and drink, the traditional chile to enliven the fare and pulque to wash it down.

The religion of the people is basically Roman Catholic, with a nice old colonial church dominating the *plaza*, and with the usual traditional round of *fiestas* to mark the passing of the agricultural year. But there are still many pagan survivals in curing and magic and in the customs pertaining to birth and other stages of the life cycle. As late as 1927, the Aztec language, Nahuatl, was spoken by nearly all the villagers, although most of them also spoke Spanish.

But modernity intrudes in the shape of such material manifestations as mills to grind the maize, sewing machines, clocks, patent medicines, powdered milk, battery radios and even a few motor cars. A modern highway and buses now connect the village with the state capital, Cuernavaca, and from the latter it is only a step away by bus or car to Mexico City. While pool-rooms and other modern amenities have invaded the central *plaza*, in the outskirts of Tepoztlán the modern villas of rich week-enders are beginning to appear, suggesting that in the not very distant future Tepoztlán will suffer the same fate as Cuernavaca and become a residential and tourist resort.

When Lewis last examined the village in 1956 he noted many changes in the pattern of life and the outlook of the people. The

Tepoztecans seemed to him to be on the whole more outgoing and friendly and less bothered by the presence of strangers; children were noisier and smiled more; unchaperoned girls were to be seen in the streets either in groups or with their boy friends. Whereas in the old days the peasant tried to hide whatever small wealth he might have accumulated, material success and a higher standard of life were now admired and flaunted. In particular, great value was placed on education which was thought to endow its beneficiary with a higher social status. In what was before a purely peasant society there was now an incipient middle class consisting of professional men, white-collar employees and self-employed artisans and shopkeepers, whose values and goals had come to differ sharply from those of the peasantry. Many of the younger men, belonging to this more sophisticated group, had moved to the city.

So far so good, but the report ends upon a disquieting note. Lewis concluded that the peasants, who still constituted some seventy-five per cent of the population of the village, were if anything poorer than they had been in the past. Inflation had taken its toll of their meagre income. More serious, in the absence of capital, irrigation and mechanization, agriculture had stagnated; the peasants, whether working on *ejidos* or as private owners, continued to farm for subsistence and to cling to their old ways. During the Revolution the great *haciendas* in the neighbourhood had been destroyed by Zapata's armies, and the land divided among the peasants, but the second stage of agrarian reform – measures to increase productivity – seems to have by–passed Tepoztlán. Most of the benefits of modern progress have been confined to the new emergent middle class, who only indirectly live off the land, and many of whom have found better jobs outside the village.

THE PHENOMENON OF URBAN GROWTH
An overall shortage of cultivable land, the population increasing at the rate of $3\frac{1}{2}$ per cent annually (one of the highest growth-rates in the world), and a pool of some two or three million landless peasants looking for work – against such a background it is not surprising that many of the brighter young men and women in the villages, as well as some of the not so bright, have fallen for the lure of the big cities. In particular the capital, with its bright lights, tall buildings and encircling ring of factories, is a powerful magnet, attracting

rural immigrants at an ever-increasing rate estimated to be now more than one thousand a week. The result is terrifying. In 1910, when the Republic celebrated its centenary, Mexico City was a pleasant 'little Paris' with a population of 368,000. Today, according to the preliminary figures of the latest census (1970), it is a vast sprawling city of over eight million inhabitants. All the other major cities, such as Guadalajara (1,196,218), Monterrey (830,336) and Puebla (521,885), have been expanding too, but not to such an alarming extent.

With the best will in the world on the part of the authorities, cities which are growing so fast find themselves faced with the most appalling problems. The officials of the Federal District have performed wonders in promoting popular housing schemes, but it has been physically impossible to provide enough accommodation for such a large mass of immigrants, most of whom are incapable of paying an economic rent, and supplying such essential facilities as water, drainage and electricity. In a recent study[7] it was estimated that in the Mexican capital two million people do not have access to a piped water supply and one-third of the immigrant families live without a drainage system. In the slums in the centre of the city most families live, sleep and eat in one room which opens out upon a communal courtyard shared by dozens of other families. The conditions are even worse in the shanty-towns on the dry hillsides surrounding the city, where the 'parachutists', as the immigrants are popularly described, squat in misery with their numerous children and animals without any municipal services of any kind.

Oscar Lewis[8] has described, in lurid detail, based on tape-recorded interviews with each member of an immigrant family, the life of the people in a one-story tenement building in a slum in the heart of Mexico City. The father of the family, Jesús Sánchez, was a peasant born in a small village in the state of Vera Cruz in 1910, the year which marked the beginning of the Mexican Revolution. 'We always lived in one room, like the one I live in today, just one room. We all slept there, each on his little bed made of boards and boxes. In the morning, I would get up and make the sign of the cross. I washed my face and my mouth and went to haul the water. After breakfast, if they didn't send me for wood, I would sit in the shade. Usually I would take a *machete* and rope and would go into the countryside to look for dry wood. I came back carrying a huge bundle on my back. That was my work when I lived at home. I worked since I was very small. I knew nothing of games.' Jesús ran away from home when he was about twelve years old, doing odd jobs on the sugar plantations and in a grain mill and later migrating to Mexico City. Here he finally settled down in a job which was to last him for the rest of his life as a food buyer for a small restaurant, earning a wage of 12.50 pesos a day (the equivalent then of about one US dollar). He could hardly support his family on this amount and supplemented his income by selling lottery tickets, and by raising and selling pigs, pigeons, chickens and singing birds.

The children, Manuel, Roberto, Consuelo and Marta were born between 1928 and 1935 in the slums of Mexico City. They did not have a happy childhood. Their mother died when they were young, and their father was a hard disciplinarian, anxious for his children to get ahead in the world, but with no tolerance for human failings. He exerted his authority in the old-fashioned manner with a belt, and was both loved and feared by his sons; a young step-mother, not much older than the daughters, did not add to the harmony of the family circle. The physical conditions in the tenement were grim, with more than one married couple usually occupying the same bedroom; in the absence of any privacy the inmates were forced to live most of their lives out in the streets. The boys formed themselves into gangs, and there was a lot of fighting, for among the Mexicans the quality of *machismo* (manliness) is greatly admired. Sexual life was precocious, with free unions and the inevitable crop of unwanted and ill-cared-for children. The men were usually broke and drifted from one ill-paid job to another. When they did have money they would spend it on drink, gambling and expensive clothes or gadgets, without putting any money aside for a rainy day.

Actually, the Sánchez children had a better start in life than many of their neighbours. Jesús was a good provider; there was always food in the house, and the family even had a radio. Whereas the father had had only one year of schooling, all the children spent several years in primary school, and one of the girls, Consuelo, graduated from primary school and completed two years of commercial school as well. But none of them benefited from their education. Roberto, the bad hat of the family, spent some time in the army and did a spell in jail. Manuel wandered from one unsatisfactory job to another and for a time worked in the markets, dealing in second-hand stuff – clothes,

shoes, gold, silver, watches, furniture, anything that came along –
but he only made enough money out of his dealings to cover the bare
expenses of food and drink. The girls drifted from one unfortunate
love affair to another.

The depressing conclusion of this book is that, while the father,
who had been brought up as a peasant in the Porfirian tradition of
authoritarianism, with its emphasis upon knowing one's place, hard
work and self-abnegation, managed to raise himself out of the lower
depths of poverty, his post-Revolutionary children, in spite of their
much better opportunities, never made anything out of their lives
and remained in poverty. The father summed it up thus: 'My sons
haven't amounted to anything because they don't like to have
anyone order them around. First, they want to be millionaires and then
get a job. How can you expect to start from the top? We all have to
work our way up from the bottom, isn't that so? But my sons, they
want to do it the other way round. So everything that they do is a
failure. They don't have any stamina for work. They don't have the
will-power to get a job and stick to it, an honest job so that they can
go out in the street looking decent and feeling proud of themselves'.

The Children of Sánchez is required reading for the student of 'the
culture of poverty', a social phenomenon which is to be found in all
the great cities of the world, and even in countries of great wealth
which have far less excuse for it than Mexico. A society in such rapid
transition as that of Mexico is bound to produce the kind of conditions
which Lewis describes. But is the Sánchez family typical? There must
be many other similarly poor families (I have personal knowledge of
a number of such cases) in which at least one of the sons or daughters
had the will-power and character to break out of the circle of poverty
into the promised land of the middle class. This is proved by the
statistics quoted at the beginning of this chapter. As another American
writer has put it:

Nearly every society for which we have any historical or present
record retains a body of underprivileged. Probably about a third
of the Mexican population will so remain for many years to come.
But this is fewer by half than at the end of the Díaz period. The
Revolution has achieved one of its aims. Society is 'open'. In
technical jargon, status is 'achieved', not ascribed; what a man does,
rather than who his father was, is the main determinant of status.
Moreover, nearly half of the Mexican people have risen in the

social and economic scale since 1910, some to undreamed-of heights. The humblest and poorest can now aspire to having a son or daughter at a university, perhaps even winning a scholarship abroad. This is now almost a real expectancy of the new middle class, which has tripled under the Institutional Revolution.[9]

THE ECONOMIC BACKGROUND

In his inaugural speech as a presidential candidate, Echeverría uttered a warning to his countrymen against making a cult of economic growth and regarding it as an end in itself. The objective of economic policy, he said, should be essentially humanitarian – to bring about the most rapid improvement in the conditions of life of the people as a whole. There are two basic requirements. First the growth rate must be substantially in excess of the annual rate of population increase (3.5 per cent); otherwise there can be no over-all progress at all. Second, economic growth must be balanced between the rural and urban sectors of the economy, with the increase in industrial capacity and production matched by a corresponding improvement in agricultural productivity; otherwise the benefits of any growth will be unevenly distributed, perpetuating and increasing those undesirable structural distortions in the economy which have produced the phenomenon of rural poverty side by side with urban affluence, and the consequential mass migration of peasants to the cities at a faster rate than they can be absorbed.

In meeting the first requirement – over-all growth – Mexico has been remarkably successful during the last thirty years. Real gross national product has grown since 1940 at a compound annual rate of some 6 per cent and has been close to 7 per cent in recent years. Over-all average per capita income has advanced at about 3 per cent per annum. This achievement is all the more impressive when one considers that Mexico entered the 1940's in a less favourable position than most developing countries. The chaos resulting from almost a decade of revolution so retarded economic growth that it was not until the mid-1930's that real per capita income reached pre-1910 levels. Remarkable too, if one bears in mind the heavy inflation suffered by the economies of most Latin American countries, is Mexico's unparalleled record of price and exchange stability. The peso has maintained its value of $0.08 since 1954, and the consumer price level has risen in the past decade at an annual rate of only 2.6

per cent. The Mexican peso is now one of the world's hardest currencies and has given the Mexican government a credit rating strong enough to place large bond issues in the New York and other money markets at favourable rates of interest.[10] So strong is it that the Mexican peso is today listed among those hard currencies used by the International Monetary Fund to bolster up the currencies of countries which find themselves in balance of payments difficulties, such as Britain experienced in 1967. This is in striking contrast with the situation in the nineteenth century, when Mexico, in chronic default on her foreign debt, was a bad word in the City of London.

The second basic requirement – balanced growth – still remains to be achieved. The pattern of growth during the last sixty years has been characterized by relative stagnation in agricultural productivity, except on the efficient farms, accompanied by what can only be described as an industrial revolution. In 1910 Mexico was still almost entirely an agricultural country. Today manufacturing output accounts for more than a quarter of GNP, with services and commercial activities representing another 40 per cent. Whereas, in the days of Porfirio Díaz, virtually all consumer goods were imported and only within reach of the purse of a small minority of the population, now the shops in Mexican cities are full of locally made consumer goods of every kind – Mexico is even making her own motor cars.

Among individual industries which have experienced rapid growth in recent times chemicals stand out as one of the most dynamic, with an expanding production of caustic soda, chlorine, fertilizers, petrochemicals and pharmaceuticals. Mexico is today the world's leading supplier of hormones with six companies producing enough to fill about half the world demand. Pemex, the government-owned oil corporation, is currently engaged in a major expansion programme, not only in the field of petrochemicals, but in drilling, refining and distribution to keep pace with the growth in domestic demand for petroleum products and natural gas. One of the oldest, largest and most successful of Mexico's industries is steel production, which began in Monterrey in 1903 and is still centred in that city and nearby Monclava. The steel plants are ideally situated to take advantage of local resources, making use of the coking coal from northern Coahuila, iron ore from Durango and manganese from northwestern Chihuahua. Although the mining industry has not been booming in recent years, Mexico is rich in mineral resources, ranking among the world's largest producers of silver, sulphur, lead and zinc and also producing substantial quantities of gold and copper in addition to the coal, iron and manganese mentioned above. The mining industry employs over 50,000 workers and produces an output valued annually at more than 300 million dollars, much of which is exported. Finally, mention should be made of the impressive expansion of the infrastructure. A lot of money has been spent on modernizing the national railways and building motor highways. During the period 1950–68 electrical generating capacity – Mexico is rich in hydro-electrical resources – has been increased five-fold.

All this represents a remarkable achievement. But unfortunately the economic benefits of industrialization have been confined to only a part of the population: many enterprising Mexicans have made fortunes out of their factories; the unionized workers in industry belong to an aristocracy compared to the peasants and the general run of the urban proletariat; shopkeepers and other middle men have likewise profited. In short, industrialization and urban affluence are two sides of the same coin. Herein lies the root cause of the lack of balance in the country's economy. Industry, as it has grown up so far, is much too heavily concentrated in a few favoured spots. For example, Mexico City and its environs in the Federal District is so overloaded with industry that it accounts for no less than 43 per cent of Mexico's gross national product. True, there is now a tendency for industry to spill over from the Valley of Mexico to the outskirts of neighbouring cities such as Puebla, Toluca and Cuernavaca. For example, Volkswagen have built their new assembly plant near Puebla; General Motors and Chrysler-Dodge have established plants outside Toluca; Ford have a factory in Cuautitlán off the main highroad leading out of Mexico City towards the north. Essentially, however, this outward movement of industry represents no more than the spreading of the tentacles of the capital over a wider but still highly concentrated complex of urban and industrial areas situated in the heart of Mexico.

Further afield the only major industrial centres are Monterrey (brewing, steel, textiles, glass, paper etc.) and Guadalajara, where much of the economic development is based on processing local products and manufacturing goods for the regional market. There are also some important new industries in the far north on the Mexican side of the US border, in which relatively cheap Mexican labour is used to process manufactures destined for sale in the US market. The oil industry is mostly concentrated in the tropical areas of the Gulf Coast from Tampico downwards, and there are now important petrochemical plants in Vera Cruz and Tabasco. But these provincial centres of industry are like oases in a desert. There are still vast areas of the country, especially in the south, which are virtually lacking in industry of any sort; and it is in those regions that the phenomenon of rural poverty is at its worst. The de-centralization of industry, and the development of rural industry, figure prominently in the plans of the new government.

So rapid a transformation of Mexico from an agricultural to a semi-industrial society would not have been possible without the active support and stimulation of successive Mexican governments. Not only were the new-born industries protected from foreign competition by high tariff walls, and assisted by other incentives to the private sector, but the government itself became a major shareholder in many of the new enterprises, with complete control over the railways, oil and the supply of electrical energy and with a stake, through the official development bank, Nacional Financiera, in a large assortment of industries, including iron and steel, foodstuffs and automobiles. There are some business men in Mexico who criticize this massive intrusion of the government into industry; such critics resent the fat jobs in the state enterprises which are filled by loyal party supporters, and claim that many of the new industries are uneconomic; the Mexican public, they assert, is forced to pay inflated prices for goods which are often shoddy in comparison with their foreign counterparts. The Mexican government has shown itself to be aware of these shortcomings, and there are indications that official attitudes are beginning to retreat somewhat from the high tariff policy of the past. But there is no retreat in sight from the active participation of the government in the economic life of the country. Modern Revolutionary Mexico is firmly wedded to Alemán's doctrine of a mixed economy. Basically the issue is one of nationalism versus the old-fashioned doctrine of free trade. As one Mexican business man put it to me: the Mexican people dearly love to see the Mexican flag flying over their factories; but whenever they get the chance they cannot resist slipping over the border to do their shopping!

Thanks to the Revolution, the Mexican flag does now fly proudly on virtually every factory in the country, as well as over the railways and oilfields where foreigners once ruled the roost. Foreign investment has played an important part in the modern development of Mexico but under conditions of national control and regulation which were conspicuously lacking in the time of Díaz. The total US private investment in Mexico was estimated to be $1,459,000,000 in 1968, and new money from a wide variety of countries is entering the republic for investment in Mexican enterprises at a rate of some 100 to 200 million dollars a year. But 'economic imperialism', as the Mexicans experienced it in the time of Díaz, is now a thing of the past. Foreign concerns seeking to do business in Mexico have the choice of establishing wholly owned subsidiaries or entering into joint ventures or licensing agreements with Mexican business concerns. The Mexican government usually frowns upon the first possibility, and requires or encourages majority Mexican interest in the latter. Thus there is a growing tendency for foreign interests to prefer licensing arrangements, selling to Mexico their techniques or designs in return for the payment of royalties.

In spite of their high cost structure, 29 per cent of Mexican exports now consist of manufactured goods, the balance consisting of agricultural products (just over half the total) and minerals, while tourism has become an important item on the revenue side of the balance of payments. Mexico being more or less self-sufficient in food, imports consist largely of capital goods and raw materials. As in all developing countries, the value of imports exceeds exports. The deficit on current account is covered by foreign investment and the government's borrowing abroad, which increased by over 60 per cent between 1962 and 1967. This mounting foreign debt is clearly something which requires careful watching. But the Mexicans have shown themselves to be very prudent in their economic policy, and, as we saw, Mexico's credit abroad stands very high. In 1967 the servicing of Mexico's foreign debt represented no more than 2.6 per cent of the productive capacity of the country and is therefore well within the capacity of the country to pay.

All in all, then, the Mexicans have every reason to feel proud of their progress in the economic field, and there is no reason to think that it will not continue, although perhaps not in the future at quite such a spectacular rate. 'Balanced growth', involving the expansion of transport, power, communications and education as well as industry, combined with a major attack upon the problems of the small uneconomic farmer, will be among the most important aims of the new Mexican government. Thus, although the children of Sánchez failed to make good in their slum environment, there is every reason to hope that at least some of the numerous grandchildren of Jesús Sánchez will find a niche in the affluent society of the new Mexico. In such a rapidly expanding economy, and with society in a state of flux, opportunities should abound for the younger generation of Mexicans. Not all will benefit perhaps; but anybody with will, ability, and a bit of luck, should be able to improve his lot.

9   The people and politics

A VISITOR TO MEXICO at the beginning of 1970 might well have been puzzled by the spectacle of the PRI candidate, Luis Echeverría, actively campaigning for the presidency, although in the certain knowledge that, barring an act of God, he was bound to be elected. If there was no doubt about the result of the election, why all the speeches? Why the posters on every street corner with the slogan 'Arriba y Adelante con Echeverría', (upward and forward with Echeverría) or the huge placards on the highways outside every town proclaiming that Puebla, Cuernavaca, or whatever the place might be, was firmly supporting the official candidate? But, as we shall see, this is a superficial impression; there is in fact a valid explanation of what at first sight might seem to be a nonsense.

To understand contemporary Mexican politics it is essential to grasp that the Mexican Revolution has evolved its own unique brand of democracy, which is different in many respects from British or North American practice, as indeed also from what the liberal authors of the Constitution of 1857 – the Constitution for which Madero fought so passionately – intended the Mexican political system to be. The liberal formula, copied from Anglo-Saxon models, failed to produce good results in Mexico over a period of a century, and Madero too was unable to make it work. In contrast, the political system described below is based on Mexican realities; it has given the country forty years of stable and progressive government, and is the envy of other Latin American republics. It deserves, therefore, to be examined objectively.

According to the Constitution, Mexico is a federal, democratic republic, consisting of twenty-nine States, two Federal Territories and a Federal District. The President, State Governors and members of the Federal and State Congresses are elected by direct universal suffrage,

146

and cannot be re-elected. The President is the Chief Executive of the nation and wields enormous power – not only does he perform the formal and ceremonial duties of a Head of State, but he is responsible also for the day-to-day running of the government, of which he is the unchallenged head. The Congress is composed of a Senate, made up of 60 senators (two from each State and two from the Federal District), and a Chamber of Deputies (one deputy for each 200,000 of the population or a minimum of over 100,000 for each electoral District). Congress is empowered by the Constitution to legislate in all matters affecting the national interest. The Constitution grants to the States those powers not expressly vested in the Federal Government. They have their own representative governments consisting of an elected governor, who is the Chief Executive in the State, and a Chamber of Deputies. Standing apart from the executive and legislative branches of the government, the judiciary, consisting of local and federal courts and a Supreme Court, is responsible for seeing that the constitution is upheld and the civic rights of the people safeguarded.

Such is the position on paper. But, as we saw when studying the history of Mexico in the nineteenth century, this essentially North American concept of combined presidential and congressional government, based on a separation of powers between the executive, Congress and the judiciary, never worked at all well in Mexico; indeed this has been the experience in virtually all the Latin American republics. It has no roots in Spanish practice or tradition. In nineteenth-century Mexico, with so large a proportion of the population illiterate, elections tended to be a farce. More often than not generals came into power, not through elections, but by military coups d'état. Congress, torn apart by rival political factions – an orderly two-party system on the British or US models never materialized – was often irresponsible in its actions on the rare occasions when it was allowed to function at all. State governorship tended to fall into the hands of powerful local *caciques* who either ignored or actively intrigued against the Federal government. On the pretext of saving the country from anarchy, presidents of Mexico, for the most part military men, often found it necessary to assume dictatorial powers, turning the supposedly independent Congress and the judiciary into rubber stamps, and imposing their authority, if necessary by force, upon the States. Such a system of centralized dictatorial government was perfected by Porfirio Díaz, who gave the country thirty-five years of peace, but only at the cost of consigning the democratic provisions of the constitution to the wastepaper basket.

This was the historical background against which the more hardheaded leaders of the Mexican Revolution who succeeded Madero – notably Calles, Cárdenas and Alemán – devised and perfected a new technique of democratic government, based on a single 'Revolutionary' Party, which since 1929 has dominated the political life of the country. It has given to the Mexican people the best of two worlds – the strong, centralized government which past experience has shown to be essential to avoid anarchy; but a government which is nevertheless to some extent sensitive to the will of the people. What is more, it ensures a smooth transition of power from one presidential regime to another. During the last thirty years there have been none of the armed rebellions which in the past were touched off by virtually every presidential election, and are still so much a feature of political life in most of the Latin American republics.

The term 'one-party' democracy is not strictly speaking accurate, for, as we shall see later, an opposition of sorts does exist. Basically, however, the Mexican political system depends upon a monopoly of power by a single party (PRI) which purports to represent all those elements in society – peasants, workers and middle class – which support the Revolution. The PRI has the men, the money and the vast apparatus of the State behind it, a combination of forces which makes it invincible at the polls. But although it possesses a monopoly of power, the structure of the party is democratic, at any rate in theory. It is organized functionally in three sections: an agrarian section built around the powerful peasants' confederation (CNC); a labour section based on the equally powerful Confederation of Mexican Workers (CTM) (in these two sections alone are represented some six million peasants and workers); the third, so-called 'popular', section is made up of diverse organizations representing such middle-class elements as schoolteachers, civil servants, professional men etc. Outside the organization of the Party, but supporting it, are the army, a loyal and disciplined professional force, and a large segment of the business community, many of whose members have greatly profited from the Revolution. Thus, although it is organized as a single party, the PRI is in effect a broadly based coalition of diverse political groups, each with their own competing interests, but bound together by a common loyalty to the Revolution, in the knowledge that union means strength, whereas the history of Mexico has shown that disunion, if allowed to take the form of open conflict between rival political factions, would almost certainly lead straight back to civil war and anarchy.

Under the Mexican system of democracy, then, most of the real political in-fighting takes place behind the closed doors of the PRI, and not out in the open in Congress and on the hustings as normally happens in a multi-party system of democracy. But the political struggle in Mexico is real enough, with each of the component groups of the PRI lobbying vigorously for their own particular interests and points of view. Public opinion too is able to make its influence felt to some extent. Within limits, the press is free in Mexico and often critical of the government;[1] Mexicans say what they like to each other without any fear, and indeed sometimes in the hope that Big Brother may be listening. The leaders of the PRI, like all democratic politicians, are sensitive to criticism in the press and take wry note of the jokes and the gossip.

Thus the policies of the PRI (and to some extent too the choice of the presidential candidate) which emerge at election times are the result of a careful balancing by the Party leaders of competing interests and points of view. The new president, obviously, will have the final word on policy, and to a considerable extent it will reflect his own personal outlook and style, but essentially it is pressures from the grass-roots of the Party, and more generally public opinion, which will have been the determining factor in setting the course of the government for the next six years. Thus, as in all democratic countries, government policy will be based on compromise and designed to please as wide a cross-section of the people as possible. If the government should fail to live up to its promises, the rank and file of the Party, and to a lesser extent the people generally, have the means to make their displeasure known, in the certain knowledge that every six years there will be a new president, and a completely new team of ministers and senior functionaries, who can be expected to review the policies of the government with the criticisms of the people in mind.

The presidential candidate is chosen in the following manner: the out-going president, taking account of the state of opinion both inside the Party and in the country as a whole, first of all consults with the Party leaders – ex-presidents, the heads of the peasant and labour unions and other supporting organizations – until a consensus is reached and an agreed candidate chosen. While these consultations and soundings are going on behind closed doors the still unannounced candidate is known as *el tapado* – the hidden one. Only when final agreement has been reached within the Party is his name announced to the people. The presidential campaign then begins.

So great is the hold of the PRI over the electorate that there is never any doubt about the result of the election; once selected by the Party the candidate of the PRI is bound to win. Even so, the electoral campaign, which is supported by massive publicity, serves a useful purpose. It enables the presidential candidate to meet with a wide cross-section of the people and learn about their problems at first hand. The people for their part are told about the government's plans, and enabled to take the measure of the president-to-be. Thus Echeverría, although certain of victory, took his campaign with the utmost seriousness. As Hugh O'Shaughnessy, Latin American correspondent of the *Financial Times*, reported:

> Echeverría promises to be both a veritable dynamo and an extremely well-informed leader. No one who has accompanied him on his election campaign is likely to forget the experience. For virtually 18 hours a day when he is on tour Echeverría works. Briefings, working breakfasts, speeches, visits to factories, stop-offs in the country's smallest villages, the acceptance of local petitions, more speeches, the careful wave to the assembled handfuls of people in those hamlets too small even for a whistle stop, conversations with the State Governor and local experts in the campaign bus, lunches, youth rallies, industrial rallies, homage to this or that hero of the Revolution, press conferences, the daily grind is stiff enough to fell most men not as passionately interested as 'The Candidate' in knowing his country's problems at first hand and reaching out to as many Mexicans as possible. [2]

The selection of PRI candidates for State governorship follows a somewhat different pattern, for here it is a question of reconciling federal and local interests. It is of vital importance to the president to have people in these posts upon whose loyalty he can rely. Thus it is the sitting president or the presidential candidate who has the final word in the choice of candidates for State governorships, although he will normally take soundings among the local leaders of the PRI in the State. The selected candidate may well be a local favourite son, but he must not have any pretensions to becoming an independent *cacique* in the nineteenth-century tradition; for that is how most of the revolutions against the central government were organized in the past. Not only must the State governor be personally loyal to the president, but he must be a member of the PRI; it would be considered highly dangerous for a member of an opposition party to become a regional head of state.[3]

In the case of the federal and State Congresses the situation is different, for these bodies have little real power; it is even of advantage to the PRI that some of the seats should be occupied by members of the opposition, if only in order to create the impression that they are genuinely democratic assemblies. For this reason, by a curious arrangement, the opposition parties are allocated a minimum number of seats in the Federal Chamber of Deputies irrespective of the vote.[4] But if they confer little power, the posts of Federal deputy or senator carry considerable prestige, and for an unscrupulous man they can also be lucrative. They are thus in much demand, and regarded in the PRI as prizes for loyal services to the Party. The president himself may name some of the candidates; State governors too are usually allowed to nominate a quota of their personal friends or supporters, but the bulk of the PRI candidates for Congress are chosen by the various sections of the Party. This means that every three years about 35 labour leaders and 40 odd spokesmen of the peasants become Federal deputies; the remaining seats in the lower house which belong to the PRI are reserved for members selected by the various organizations in the so-called 'popular' section.

It has been estimated that every six years there is a turnover in Mexico of approximately 18,000 elective offices and 25,000 appointive posts. This makes for political stability, since every loyal member of the PRI can expect, at some time or another, to have his moment of glory, whereas in the nineteenth century the seeker after office could usually obtain it only by overthrowing the government in power. But there is also a shady side. With only six years to go in any one office there is a strong temptation for the incumbent to make hay while the sun shines. In a number of his speeches Echeverría has stressed the importance of eliminating corruption in the administration. But it is not something which can be done in a day. The spoils system is endemic in Latin American politics, as indeed, in different forms (refined or otherwise) it is in most countries of the world.[5]

In essence, then, the Mexican formula for democratic government is a carefully contrived balance of the following contradictory elements: a very strong president armed with the fullest powers, but one whose term of office is limited to six years; virtually all the political activities of the country monopolized by a single, but very broadly based political party; State governors allowed considerable local autonomy provided that they are good Party members, and remain loyal to the President; a weak Congress in which a small tolerated opposition can criticize the government, but with no chance of unseating it; universal suffrage, but little choice for the voters, who mostly make their influence felt by other means, such as membership in trade unions or other pressure groups; a free press and other basic democratic rights of the individual, but the army and police will deal sternly with subversion – law and order must be maintained.

In theory, and no doubt also in some aspects of its practice, it is possible to pick all sorts of holes in the system; its pragmatic justification is that it works; it has shown itself to be well suited to Mexican conditions. It has the great merit of providing for both flexibility and continuity in government policy. As examples of flexibility one only has to recall how, when Calles became too conservative for the popular taste, he was replaced peacefully by the more revolutionary Cárdenas; after the excitements and excesses of the Cárdenas regime the country was given a much-needed rest by the more moderate Avila Camacho; Alemán, who pushed forward too vigorously with industrialization at the expense of the immediate interests of the workers and peasants, was replaced by a series of presidents who, responding to public opinion, have sought to steer a middle course between economic development and social justice. And to take a current example, there are signs that the new president, Luis Echeverría, has been chosen by his Party, presumably at the prompting of the peasant section, in response to a widespread feeling in the country that the greatest unresolved problem of the Revolution is that of the backward countryside.

But while there have been changes in emphasis from one presidential regime to another there has also been continuity; the basic policies of the Revolution have remained the same over forty years; agrarian reform, industrialization, social justice and education. Progress under the first two heads has already been described, and it only remains to be said that there have been impressive advances as well in the development of the social services and in education. For example, in all the recent Federal budgets education has outranked defence; there are today more teachers than soldiers in Mexico.[6]

Thus, whatever foreign critics may say about it, most Mexicans, especially those in their middle years and now occupying the most important positions in society, are well content with their system of government. In the eyes of the faithful the PRI is much more than an ordinary political party; as its name implies, it is regarded as a national institution – the custodian of the sacred principles of the Revolution laid down in the Constitution of 1917, to which the whole country is supposed to be dedicated. Therefore, say the faithful, to be against the PRI is to be against the Revolution. To be against the Revolution is to be against Mexico. Hence all good citizens should vote for Echeverría!

THE OPPOSITION PARTIES

Even so, there are quite a number of Mexicans, young and old, who for various reasons are hostile to the PRI, though this may not necessarily mean that they disapprove of what the Revolution has done for the country. There is a growing number of people, especially in the younger generation, who consider that the system of one-party domination is undemocratic; that the PRI has gone on for too long, is too set in its ideas, and has lost touch with the people. At the other extreme there are still a few mostly elderly people who regard the PRI as being too radical; such people often have bitter memories of the religious persecution under Calles, or they may have been deprived of their ancestral estates. Marxist intellectuals, of course, take the opposite view and consider the Revolution to be much too bourgeois and conservative. Some of the students dream of the day when there will be a second Mexican Revolution, on Castroite lines, with bearded young men of the middle class leading the peasants and workers to the barricades.[7]

There are difficulties, however, about organizing an effective opposition group in Mexico. With the PRI occupying most of the middle ground in politics, ranging from the organized peasants and workers to a large segment of the middle class, there is very little room left for manoeuvre. To attempt to compete with the PRI on its own ground is useless. An opposition party which keeps within the law and advocates moderate policies can never hope to win a presidential election. At the best it may win a few seats in Congress; its function will be confined to that of criticism, without any hope of office – not a very exciting prospect for an ambitious politician. Moreover if the criticism is constructive in all probability the PRI will adopt the idea as its own. 'If you can't beat them, join them' is a reasonable conclusion, therefore, for an aspiring politician of moderate views to reach. On the other hand, to move out to the fringe of politics, either on the extreme right or the extreme left, is fraught with peril. The politician who does so will probably find himself outside the law. Against such a strongly entrenched government as that of Mexico, with a loyal army and a tough police, a policy of violence or subversion has little prospect of success in the short or medium term. Should disorder ever become widespread, and the PRI discredited, the most likely result would be a military take-over.[8]

What might be called the respectable or tolerated opposition consists of three parties, two of which, however, are of little importance. For example, *Partido Auténtico de la Revolución* (PARM), which had six seats in the Congress of 1969, is little more than an association of elderly generals who fought in the revolutionary wars, but feel that they have little in common with the new generation of civilian bureaucrats who now control the Party. *Partido Popular Socialista* (PPS) is likewise a breakaway party, but on the extreme left. It consists of the supporters of the now deceased former head of the CTM, Lombardo Toledano. This splinter group of the left looks to Moscow for its inspiration. But it is completely overshadowed by the much more powerful left wing of the PRI which was led by Cárdenas. In 1970, for want of a candidate of their own, the PPS, which has 10 seats in the Congress, supported Echeverría.

The only even approximately effective opposition party, with 20 seats in the Congress, is *Partido Acción Nacional* (PAN). This party came into being in 1939 around a nucleus of conservative business and professional men and other elements who were disturbed by the radical policies of Cárdenas. Its historical background is therefore conservative, and indeed, in the early days, it was suspected of having clerical backing. But under its present leader, Efrain González Morfín, PAN is trying to acquire the new look of a party representing the middle class, and with a more progressive outlook on social questions than that of the PRI. If PAN can successfully create such an image and thereby increase its support on a national scale, it could fulfil a useful national purpose by subjecting the PRI in Congress to a barrage of constructive criticism and thus keeping that august and mammoth organization on its toes. Complacency is the greatest single danger in a one-party system of government.

THE STUDENTS AND YOUTH

The PRI is also faced by the growing problem of the generation gap. The old soldiers who fought in the revolutionary wars are fast disappearing. Their sons, mostly comfortably-off bureaucrats and business men, have taken over the reins of power, and are well content with their lot, and proud of what the Revolution has achieved. But what of the third generation – the young men and women now in their twenties who will shortly be leaving the university and embarking upon their careers? Brought up in comfortable homes with all the advantages of the technocratic society which the Revolution has created, or perhaps the fortunate sons of working men, these young people take for granted the remarkable achievements of the Revolution, upon which their fathers congratulate themselves, seeing only the still glaring inequalities in society and the vast amount of work which remains to be done in order to turn the Constitution of 1917 into reality. The old rousing party slogans have little magic for the younger generation – Villa and Zapata have become disembodied mythical heroes. Many of the young regard with cynicism a so-called 'revolutionary' organization which is dominated by party elders, not only in the Party itself but in the workers and peasant unions, holding back the younger men, who if they could rise to the top, might bring in some fresh ideas.

According to the census of 1970 the majority of Mexicans today are 18 years old or younger; and the eighteen-year-olds have been given the vote. Thus the growing dissatisfaction of Mexican youth with the *status quo* is likely to become more and more important politically as Mexico enters the decade of the 1970's. While the problems of the peasantry are likely to be given the top priority in official policy, the most pressing political problem with which Echeverría is likely to be faced during his presidency is that of harnessing the idealism of youth to the ageing chariot of the PRI; of channelling youthful energies into productive enterprises, instead of allowing them to be dissipated in angry protest such as characterized the students' riots in 1968.

It is not easy for the would-be objective observer, asking questions a year after the event, to establish exactly what happened during that bloody battle between soldiers and students which took place in Tlatelolco on 2 October 1968. The students certainly had some legitimate grievances on purely academic grounds – poor teaching, swollen classes and little individual attention from their mentors in universities which have been built up too rapidly, with the worthy object of extending the benefits of higher education to a wider sector of the population. But the root cause of the troubles was political. In Mexico, as elsewhere in the world, there is to be found among the students an incoherent sense of grievance against the establishment. But it is only a minority of students who hold extreme views and resort to violence.

A recent sampling of student opinion in Mexico by a Harvard team[9] (the students were asked to define their attitude towards Fidel Castro, the USA etc.) showed that out of 830 Mexican students interviewed (90 per cent in the University of Mexico and 10 per cent in a provincial university) 33 per cent belonged to the right wing in politics, 50 per cent occupied the middle of the road, and only 17 per cent subscribed to left-wing views. But in student politics it is the extremist tail which wags the dog. The Mexican Government claim that the students were armed and organized by foreign (presumably Castroite?) agitators, in a deliberate attempt to blacken the country's reputation, just when the eyes of the world were focussed on Mexico at the time of the Olympic Games. By some means, certainly, the cadres of hard-core student militants had managed to equip themselves with automatic rifles, and they seemed to have a lot of money at their disposal for propaganda.

The students' manifestation on 2 October was peaceful until the Mexican army advanced upon the plaza in force in order to arrest the leaders. According to a report in the New York *Times* sent by a Mexican eye-witness, Ambassador Jorge Castañeda, armed guerrillas began the fighting by opening fire on the advancing troops from an upper window; the army retaliated with machine guns and two hundred people were killed in the fight. Whatever may be the true facts, this incident greatly shocked world opinion and did a great deal of harm to the reputation of the Mexican government, from which it has never fully recovered. Most members of the Mexican establishment, while deploring the bloodshed, support the government's contention that 'foreign subversion' had to be dealt with severely. But it would be difficult to find a young person in Mexico who is not bitterly critical of the government's action. Both in Mexico and abroad deep concern is felt about the fate of the student leaders who, in early 1970, were still languishing in jail without trial. Many young people regard them as martyrs.

Student unrest in Mexico is symptomatic of the revolutionary ground-swell which is to be found today all over Latin America, as indeed also in many other parts of the world. While their problems are very different (Mexico is far from being an affluent society, and family ties are still extremely strong), the young people of Mexico are increasingly copying the long hair, styles of dress and social and political attitudes of youth in the USA. In politics, the more moderate Mexican youths merely yearn for a greater measure of democracy and social justice (without perhaps thinking very clearly about how these things are to be attained). But among the extremists the youthful ideal is the Castroite guerrilla fighter. And with the example in other countries of so many successful acts of terrorism – bomb explosions, hi-jackings and the seizing and murder of hostages – there is a grave danger that the cult of violence will spread in Mexico.

Political unrest in Mexico is still vague and without specific objectives, but under competent leadership it could become dangerous. In the slums of the great cities and in the lower ranks of the labour unions and peasant organizations there must be quite a lot of inflammable material, only waiting for a spark to set it alight.

Thus the youthful desire for a renovation of political life is the most important challenge which faces the PRI as it enters the decade of the 1970's. Many of the leaders of the PRI have shown themselves to be aware of the need for change, but there are also some strongly entrenched conservatives in the Party who would like things to remain as they are. Thus when the late Carlos Madrazo, a former chairman of the Party, went too far and too fast for the taste of his more conservative colleagues, in introducing democratic reforms, he was dismissed from his post. Echeverría has stated frequently in public that the PRI should subject itself to the most searching examination. But he has also uttered this warning: if it embarks upon reform, the Party must be careful not to weaken the structure of an institution which has been built upon the foundations of historical experience, and has served the country well during the last forty years.

10   The intellectual and social climate

IN ITS BROADER ASPECTS the Mexican Revolution can be seen as the culmination of a process of racial and cultural integration which began, figuratively, on that fateful night when Hernán Cortés took as his mistress the Indian maiden, La Malinche, thus setting the fashion among his companions for an intermingling of the two ancestral races to which modern Mexico owes its birth. From that time onwards miscegenation (the physical merging of the two races) moved steadily forward, so that now probably something like three-quarters of the Mexican people are of mixed Spanish and Indian blood. But the rigid hierarchical structure of colonial society, which persisted during the first century of the republic, kept the two cultures apart. It was only after the lapse of four centuries, when the essentially European-style superstructure of the Díaz regime crumbled and fell, that the real Mexico began to emerge with a cultural identity of its own. In the words of the Mexican poet, Octavio Paz, the Revolution was 'a discovery of our own selves, a return to our origins'.[1]

It is true that, while Díaz still sat in the presidential chair, a new generation of Mexican intellectuals, which included such outstanding figures as Antonio Caso and Alfonso Reyes, had begun to question the prevailing doctrine of positivism, with its emphasis upon science and material progress, and its lack of human sympathy for the plight of ordinary people. At this time, too, a few lone anarchists and socialists, living in constant fear of the police, were also preaching revolutionary doctrines. But in its intellectual causes and consequences, the Mexican Revolution was much more than a mere revolt by a few professors against an unpopular political philosophy, or the result of isolated extremist agitation. It was more like the eruption of a volcano. Like molten lava, a flood of strong nationalistic feeling swept through the nation, directed against foreign domination of every kind – the control of foreigners over the means of production; foreign fashions and ways of thought; and, by extension, it was aimed too against the hated *científicos*, who, as people saw it, were working hand in glove with foreigners, if not actually in their pay. At a deeper level the eruption was the release of long pent-up desires for self-expression by the submerged Indian and mestizo segments of the population, representing the majority of the people.

Thus, while the revolutionary armies, and the governments which they put into power, were tearing down the pillars of the Porfirian establishment, the intellectuals were likewise engaged upon a gigantic task of demolition and renovation, discarding foreign influences, and digging down into the rich mine of Mexico's own culture and experience for new inspiration. The result was an efflorescence in all branches of learning and the arts, handicrafts, painting, literature, poetry, philosophy, archeology, anthropology, architecture, music, and even in such fields as the cinema.[2] It was a national renaissance.

In its ideology the Revolution, which started under Madero as no more than a liberal demand for a return to democratic government, soon developed into a revolt of underprivileged Indian peasants (and to a lesser extent of mestizo industrial workers) against their white masters. It became in part a racial conflict; hence the tendency in modern Mexico, already noted in an earlier chapter, to exalt the pre-Columbian past and the Indian strain in the Mexican heritage. Antedating as it did the Russian Revolution, the Mexicans see their own Revolution as being an indigenous phenomenon. But, of course, once it had started, the communists tried to cash in, equating the Indian peasants with the Marxist proletariat, and casting the white upper class in the role of capitalistic exploiters. Many of the more radical Mexican intellectuals subscribe to Marxist or near Marxist views, are strongly anti-American and prone to sympathize with the Communist powers.[3]

With politics so much coloured by the struggle between Indians and whites, not unnaturally the cultural renaissance, which the Revolution provoked, was strongly indigenist in its orientation; this comes out clearly in the literature and the art of the period between Madero's uprising and the presidency of Cárdenas. The Mexicans began to look with new eyes upon the crumbling temples of the Maya and Toltec past, with their splendid sculptures and associated works of art, which for centuries had been ignored except by a handful of experts. The humble arts and crafts of the villages – the pottery, tapestries, wood carvings, leather-work, and so on – were likewise suddenly rediscovered. In his two beautifully illustrated folio volumes, *Las Artes Populares en México*, the Mexican painter and poet, Dr Atl (born as Gerardo Murillo, he adopted an Indian name), presented to his countrymen in 1922 a breath-taking panorama of Mexican village folk art, which was to serve as an inspiration to Mexican artists during the next twenty years.

Mention has already been made of the three famous Mexican painters, Orozco, Rivera and Siqueiros, whose tremendous works adorn the walls of many of the public buildings of Mexico. Making use of the wonderful colours of the Mexican countryside, and with their themes mostly drawn from the revolutionary struggle, these great murals reflect the nationalistic and indigenist spirit of this period of Mexican history. Their realism is in striking contrast with the polite, drawing-room paintings, in European styles, of the nineteenth-century Mexican painters. They breathe the spirit of resurgent Mexico, cruel and harsh in their caricatures of the wicked *conquistadores*, landowners and the subservient priests who had exploited the people, but with profound sympathy shown for the Indian under-dog, who is depicted stoically undergoing every kind of agony, torture, the lash, or merely, like the *burro*, carrying huge loads on bent and weary backs. Nor are these three alone in their glory. There is a whole school of Mexican painters, many of them with outstanding talent, of the same period, but whose names are less well known internationally. In art these sudden outbursts of creative activity usually come in waves; the Mexico of the 1920's was no exception to the rule.

In literature, too, the Revolution produced a crop of Mexican writers, who, abandoning the flowery literary tradition of the nineteenth-century, set down in terse prose, reminiscent of Hemingway or Steinbeck, the tremendous story of the Revolution, with the emphasis on the grim nature of the struggle, and the cruelty of man to man. Probably the two most outstanding novels of the period were Mariano Azuela's *Los de Abajo* (The Under-dogs) and Martin Luis Guzman's *El Aguila y la Serpiente* (The Eagle and the Serpent), which was based on the life of Pancho Villa. The author did not glamorize his hero, as is the modern fashion among Mexican writers; the book tells with stark realism the story of the revolutionary fighting, with its cruel shooting of prisoners and other horrors, but never forgetting the human anxieties of the little men who found themselves caught up in this gigantic affray. 'Revolution', Azuela wrote, 'is like a hurricane which carries you along as if you were a dead leaf.'

Another group of writers, more directly 'indigenist' in their outlook, based their novels on the problems of the Indians when brought into contact with white civilization. For example, in his novel *El Indio* (1935), Gregorio López y Fuentes described the miseries brought upon an Indian community by a band of white men searching for gold. Or again in his novel *Juan Pérez Jolote* (1952) Ricardo Pozas tells the story of an Indian from Chiapas, who was caught up in the revolutionary armies, where he picks up Spanish and mestizo ways, but finally retires in disgust once more to his native village, where he is treated as a foreigner.[4]

In this context it is pertinent to mention the works of some of the outstanding North American authors, of liberal leanings, who in the 1920's and 1930's did a great deal to publicize the Mexican Revolution in the USA and throughout the English speaking world. The great classic, still very much worth reading, is Ernest Gruening's *Mexico and Its Heritage* (1928) which contains perhaps the most crushing indictment of the Porfirian dictatorship that has ever been written. Eyler N. Simpson's *The Ejido, Mexico's Way Out* (1937) is an idealistic account of the agrarian problem in Mexico – the future of Mexico, he thought, lay in the communal *ejidos*. With modernization of their methods of farming, arrangements made for the co-operative marketing of their crops, and with the development of local crafts and industries, the *ejidos*, Simpson foresaw, would become the nuclei around which to build a happy and prosperous Mexico, in which the Indians could expect to enjoy the good life. Frank Tannenbaum's *Peace By Revolution* (1933) likewise contains a sympathetic description of the aims of the Revolution, with its emphasis on agrarian and labour reform and education as the spear-heads of the attack. All these books are strongly indigenist in their slant, and envisage the development of a still predominantly rural Mexico, in which Indian and European culture and values would be merged, to the advantage of the Mexican people as a whole.

So wrote the pundits thirty or forty years ago, little realizing (and how could they foresee it?) that in 1970 half of the Mexican population would be living in cities, while in the countryside the Utopian prospect of happy and prosperous village communities would still be, for the most part, an unrealized dream. Tannenbaum's 'philosophy of little things' has been superseded by large-scale industrialization. It is no doubt because things have turned out so differently from what was envisaged that there is a tendency among modern Mexican and foreign writers to have second thoughts about the Revolution, and to ask in what direction it is leading the country.

One such disillusioned Mexican is José Vasconcelos, who as Minister of Education in the government of Obregón threw himself with such fervour into the task of building village schools, in 1929 stood unsuccessfully for the presidency against the Callista nominee, Ortiz Rubio, and finally retired in disgust into exile abroad. While the indigenists tended to over-glamorize the Indians and denigrate the Spaniards, Vasconcelos had a passionate belief in the Spanish heritage. In his book *La Raza Cósmica* (1925) he developed the theory that *mestizaje* – the mingling of Spanish and Indian blood – would produce the 'cosmic race' of the future. But the culture of the 'cosmic' Mexicans would be essentially Spanish, rather than Indian; it was the Latin culture, as transmitted by Spain, which would provide the gateway for the Indians into the future. His enthusiasm for Spain, strengthened by his return to the Roman Catholic faith, led Vasconcelos into hostility towards the United States of America, whose materialistic culture he abhorred. The final parting of the ways was when he supported the Axis during the war, whereas the Mexican Revolutionary government under Avila Camacho stoutly defended the cause of the Allies and drew Mexico into a close alliance with the USA. Thus the one-time revolutionary became the intellectual leader of that minority of reactionary Mexicans – there are still a few to be found today – who looked back with nostalgia to Spain and regarded the Indians as an inferior race. It was this attitude of mind among conservatives and clerics which produced the fascist phenomenon of Sinarquismo, which came to a head in the late 1930's in opposition to the radical policies of Cárdenas.

But it is not only on the extreme right of Mexican politics that there is fear of the encroachment of Anglo-Saxon values, and more generally of the materialism of the modern industrial world. For example, in his novel *La Región Más Transparente* (1958) Carlos Fuentes, one of the most outstanding of the new generation of Mexican writers, scans all the levels of modern society and is disturbed by the materialism, self-seeking and loneliness to be found in the midst of a society now able to produce a surplus of goods. He deplores the Mexican tendency to bow to foreign values. A similar fear of materialism, and dislike of the USA, is to be found in the writings of the Mexican philosopher Leopoldo Zea. Mexico, he complains, having thrown off the shackles of Spain, has become a colony of the USA. The essays in *Magia y Cibernetica* (1959) to which Zea contributed, are a latter-day adaptation of José Enrique Rodó's (a nineteenth century Uruguayan writer) famous confrontation between Ariel and Caliban, and plead for the retention of basic humanistic values ('magic') in the face of industrialization ('cybernetics').[5]

Another favourite theme of modern Mexican writers is to try to discover the true nature of the Mexican personality, split as it is between two apparently irreconcilable halves, the Indian and the Spanish. Thus Jaime Torres Bodet, a distinguished Mexican who has been a Minister of Education and was once Director General of UNESCO, has written about the wounds inflicted upon his youthful soul by the need to reconcile two warring psychologies in the Mexican nature. Other writers have commented on such phenomena as the Mexican's contempt for death. 'The sanguinary streak hits your eyes at every turn in the country's history, ancient and modern. With it goes a stoicism, even an indifference, to death in the midst of life, which seems well-nigh oriental.'[6] An Indian or Spanish trait? – it could come from either side. Pancho Villa had no compunction about seeing a man shot while he sat peacefully having his breakfast; but he was famous for his impulsive acts of kindness and generosity. Mexicans love bullfights; but they dote on children. In a fit of nihilistic despair Octavio Paz has described the Mexican's predicament in the following terms:

The strange permanence of Cortés and La Malinche in the Mexican's imagination and sensibilities reveals that they are something more than historical figures; they are symbols of a secret conflict that we have still not resolved . . . The Mexican condemns all his traditions at once, the whole set of gestures, attitudes, and tendencies in which it is now difficult to distinguish the Spanish from the Indian. For that reason the Hispanic thesis, which would have us descend from Cortés to the exclusion of La Malinche, is the patrimony of a few extremists who are not even pure whites. The same can be said of indigenist propaganda, which is also supported by fanatical Criollos and Mestizos, while the Indians have never paid it the slightest attention. The Mexican does not want to be either an Indian or a Spaniard. Nor does he want to be descended from them. And he does not affirm himself as a mixture, but rather as an abstraction: he is a man. He becomes the son of 'Nothingness'.[7]

While the poets despair, the artists too seem to have fallen into disarray. The almost religious revolutionary fervour of the great muralists has disappeared; the new school of painters who are now carrying the torch are experimenting with every kind of modern style. The Museum of Modern Art in Chapultepec Park is well worth a visit by those who like that sort of thing, but the new art does not seem to have any specifically Mexican message; much of it reflects foreign fashions. An even more agreeable way of sampling what the modern Mexican artists are producing – and some of the work is extremely good – is to visit the open-air exhibition which takes place every Sunday in a garden in Mexico City.[8] Nor should the visitor miss the weekly market, on Saturday, in San Angel a suburb of Mexico City, where the products of Mexican craftsmanship are put on display. There are some beautiful things to see and buy, even though the output is increasingly being geared to suit the taste of tourists rather than that of the Mexicans themselves. The most flourishing of the arts in Mexico today is architecture. Fine examples of modern architecture are to be seen on every side in the capital – utilitarian skyscraper blocks of offices and flats, public buildings of every shape and size, the most exotic-looking modern churches, the new National University, and private dwellings of every style. The University is a show-piece, although not perhaps to everybody's taste. My own favourite building is the new Anthropological Museum – a superb example of imaginative modern architecture. It must be one of the best laid-out museums in the world, giving the visitor, during the course of a morning or an afternoon, a complete panorama of the development of the pre-Columbian civilizations and their art. It is 'a must' for the visitor to Mexico.

So much for the intellectual and artistic ferment. Doubts and self-questioning are notably absent when one discusses the problems of Mexico with members of the ruling establishment – the leaders of the PRI, the managers of the great State corporations, the bankers and the business men – many of whom by their own efforts have managed to climb out of poverty to find a place in the affluent society. These people are full of optimism about the destiny of their country. They pin their hopes for the future on material progress based on modern technocracy. Indeed most city-bred Mexicans take pride in all the signs of the country's new-found prosperity – the expensive hotels, the skyscraper office blocks, the super-highways and the brand new metro.

The culture of the Mexican establishment is basically Spanish; but it has been modified in many subtle ways by four hundred years of evolution in the Mexican environment; it is now in the process of further modification as the result of the growth of industry and the demands of technocracy. It is this new confrontation – Ariel versus Caliban – which worries the Mexican intellectuals with hispanophile leanings. Ariel stands for the spiritual values of the Spanish heritage; Caliban stands for industry, which is associated with the USA and the Anglo-Saxon culture in the Mexican mind. Geography and history have combined to make the Mexicans the guardians of the frontier which divides the Anglo-Saxon world from the Latin world to the south of the Río Grande. The Mexicans have been faithful defenders of this frontier. They have absorbed from the USA what they needed in the way of industrial expertise, together with something of the go-getting outlook towards business of their northern neighbours. Superficial traits, such as Coca Cola, the cult of the automobile, commercial television, snack bars etc., have likewise been assimilated. But in virtually all its most important aspects the Mexican culture is intact. It may even have been fortified. For the strength of Mexican nationalism is in large part the result of proximity to the USA, and a reflection of the determination of Mexicans to preserve their heritage from foreign contamination.

The basis of this Mexican culture is the family; family loyalties in Mexico are much stronger than those abstract entities like the business in which one works or a department of government, or even the law. A Mexican would do almost anything to help a brother or a close friend. If you have the right friends or relatives in Mexico all doors will be open; there is practically nothing that cannot be arranged. The mother is the central pillar of the family. But although there is a tendency in Mexico for men to put their wives and mothers on a pedestal, and to be fierce in the defence of the honour of their daughters, women are no longer the sheltered and pampered playthings they used to be. Most Mexican girls, even from rich families, go out to work, and many of them take up professions. Chaperones are less in evidence than they used to be; not that there is any permissiveness in the upper class. Most girls acquire a *novio* by the time that they are 18 or 19, and after that they do not go out with other men. Once married the girls settle down as good mothers and usually have large families. Children are adored, and often, by English standards, spoilt; it is rare for boys or girls to be sent to a boarding-school. There is no problem of old age in Mexico. No self-respecting family in Mexico – and this applies to all classes – would let an elderly relative be sent to a public home. There is room in the house for everybody, including family retainers who have passed their prime.

Except in the café society and diplomatic set, most Mexican families prefer to confine their social activities to family gatherings (which include uncles and aunts and numerous cousins) and a circle of intimate friends. Great occasions are made out of birthdays, Saint's days, first communions, marriages and funerals. It is not easy for a foreigner to find his way into a Mexican house. Mexican business men will usually entertain their foreign clients in a club or restaurant. But if the foreigner does manage to worm his way into the charmed circle of a Mexican family he will find himself overwhelmed with attentions. There are no kinder nor more lavish hosts than the Mexicans.

The moral foundation of Mexican society is the Roman Catholic Church, which spiritually is still immensely strong, in spite of the reforms of Juárez, and the more recent persecution of the Church under Calles. Its influence is felt at all levels of society. It is an awe-inspiring experience to visit the shrine of the Virgin of Guadalupe (built on the same site as an older shrine of the Aztec earth-mother goddess) and see whole families of Indians (Guadalupe is, *par excellence*, the Indian Virgin) shuffling across the immense *plaza* on their knees, small children together with the grown-ups, and up the steps, lighted candle in hand, into the basilica. Even the children of Sánchez, brought up without much religion in a city slum, used to slip off occasionally on the long weary pilgrimage to pray to the miraculous black Christ of Chalma; such is the hold the Church still has upon the Mexican people, even though it no longer has any political power.[9] In the rich mens' suburbs the churches on Sundays are always full to overflowing, with an Indian man or woman outside selling coloured balloons for the children. The women are more regular church-goers than the men, but there are few Mexican men, even among those who have strong anti-clerical views, who will not cross themselves in a moment of crisis, or want to have a priest at their death-bed. The religious outlook of most Mexicans is conservative. Divorce and birth-control are frowned upon. Abortion would be regarded with horror in most families.

The new Mexican establishment is very far from being idle or parasitic. The men, for the most part, work extremely hard in their professions or businesses; they may start at 8 a.m. and work right through until 3 or even 4 p.m. when usually they come home for a family lunch, the principal meal of the day.[10] Back in their offices at, say, 6 p.m., they will probably work on until 8 or 9 at night. In his somewhat different way the Mexican executive is just as efficient as his Anglo-Saxon counterpart. But he has some annoying habits. He is quite likely to arrive an hour late for an appointment, with nothing but a charming smile for an excuse. *Mañana* may mean tomorrow or in three weeks' time; *un momentito* may literally be a moment or a wait of three hours – it may even mean 'never'. Mexicans are very polite people and don't like saying 'No'. In Mexican business life the 'old-boy network' is of immense importance; the foreigner seeking to do business in Mexico is well advised to find a local agent or lawyer who has the right connections.

If the Mexicans work hard, they also know how to relax. If they can afford it, they are likely to maintain a weekend house or a flat in Acapulco, or perhaps a villa in Cuernavaca. On holidays the resorts are full of pleasure-seekers – men, women and children splashing in the swimming pools or basking in the wonderful sun. Sports of every kind are very popular – golf, tennis, the Mexican ball-game (frontón), riding (European or Mexican styles), polo, water ski-ing, and all the rest. The modern young Mexican girls are as lithe, sun-burned and athletic as their brothers; they no longer grow fat in early middle age as women used to do thirty years ago. Bullfighting is still immensely popular; as for football, British television viewers do not need to be reminded that Mexico has her fans. In Central America a war has been fought over a football match!

The Mexicans of all classes like to have possessions and those who are comfortably off are proud of their luxurious houses and shining cars. The bourgeois instinct to put money into land, bricks and mortar is strong in a country in which financial stability is a recent phenomenon. It is only lately that Mexican capitalists have come round to risking their money in industrial ventures. The standard of life of the richer Mexicans seems lavish to European eyes, but this is largely because there are still servants. Even the Sánchez family, living in a slum, had a servant who came during the day to clean, do the laundry and prepare the meals.

Mexican upper-class society is prosperous, but it is fluid and open to newcomers – a man is judged by his position and wealth rather than by his family background. There is a certain amount of snobbery, of course, as in all 'society'. Members of the old families, when together in their own circles, laugh at the brash ostentation of the 'revolutionary millionaires', but they are usually glad enough to marry off their sons or daughters to the heirs of nouveau-riche parents. In the most exclusive dinner parties of bankers and diplomats Indian and mestizo faces will sometimes be seen, although upper class Mexicans pride themselves on being white. The Revolution destroyed the power of the old Creole aristocracy, but the names of the old families still figure prominently in the society pages of the newspapers. The power in Mexico has shifted from the hands of the Porfirian landed gentry into those of the technocrats, the bankers, the owners of industrial empires, the politicians, and the managers of State Corporations. In short, the new establishment in Mexico has its roots in and owes its prosperity to the Revolution; and new men are constantly emerging from the middle class to swell its ranks. It differs from the Porfirian aristocracy in one very important respect – it has a social conscience. Brought up with the ideas of the Revolution, the leaders of modern Mexico, however rich they may have become, are by no means blind to the need for social justice and reform.

11 Mexico in the modern world

MEXICO IS ONE of the 'Big Three'[1] in a bloc of 20 Latin American republics, which together have a population of some 300 million people. A friendly, stable and economically healthy Latin America is essential to the security of the USA, as indeed, but less directly, of all the countries of the Atlantic Alliance. The Latin American republics are also important internationally as holding the balance between 'East' and 'West' (or if one prefers it 'North' and 'South') in the United Nations. They occupy a half-way house between the rich and the poor countries of the world, between development and under-development, and are thus to some extent in a position to arbitrate between the two. The economic potential of Latin America is immense, at the moment, primarily as a world supplier of food and raw materials, but in the more developed countries increasingly also in industrial production. The population of Latin America is growing more rapidly than in any other part of the world. It is estimated that by the year 2000 it will have reached the astronomical figure of 556 million.[2]

In population Mexico is the largest of the Spanish-speaking countries of Latin America, being outranked in size only by Portu-guese-speaking Brazil. She is also one of the most highly industrialized of the Latin American Republics. Even so, her wealth (as measured by income per head) is considerably less than that of some of the republics, for example Argentina, which has a mainly white immi-grant population and has not been faced by the same kind of problems. In her internal structure Mexico belongs to the family of 'mestizo' countries in Central America and in the Andean area of South America which have had to cope with the problems of a mixed Indian and white population. She stands out among these republics as the country which has been most successful in solving the problems of racial and cultural integration, and, while this may not have been completely successful so far, in tackling the problem of agrarian reform. For this reason, the Mexican Revolution is greatly admired in Latin America, although none of the other countries has copied it. The Peruvian political leader Haya de la Torre modelled his revolutionary party, Apra, very much on Mexican lines, but in spite of many years of struggle, he was never able to obtain power. A military government in Peru now seems to be doing at last what Apra for so long tried to do. Could it be that President Velasco, who began his political career by expropriating a foreign oil company,[3] is destined to be the Cárdenas of Peru? This is but one of the many intriguing parallels, or contrasts, which can be drawn when comparing the history of the two countries.[4]

Mexico's foreign policy is the combined result of her geography and history. Her proximity to the USA has been the most important single factor in shaping it. During the nineteenth century Mexico lived in constant fear of US aggression and interference in her internal affairs. But now, happily, a *modus vivendi* has been reached. The Mexican border today is as safe from attack by the USA as that of Canada. Thus Mexico finds herself in the happy position of having no real problems of external security. She no longer lives in fear of military aggression on her northern border, and she herself has no motive whatsoever for attacking, or the need to defend herself against, the weak Central American republics which lie beyond her southern frontier. For this reason, unlike most of the South American republics, which bristle with arms, Mexico has been able to cut her military establishment down to a size sufficient only for maintaining internal order. Less than 10 per cent of the Mexican federal budget is spent on the armed forces.

As a defenceless country, which has no interests of her own to protect overseas, Mexico puts her faith in a policy of strict adherence to international law and treaties; she is a fierce champion of the principle that all countries, great and small, should be allowed to live their own lives, without outside interference whether from a single country or a group of countries acting collectively. Side by side with this policy of 'non-intervention', Mexico adheres to a policy of 'non-alignment', refusing steadfastly to align herself with either side in the Cold War struggle between the USA and the USSR. Some examples of the practical workings of these two policies will be given in the pages which follow.

Apart from general international questions, with which she is concerned by virtue of her membership in such bodies as the UN and the OAS, Mexico's foreign policy is mainly directed towards promoting her own economic interests. Mexico is naturally very much concerned with getting the terms of trade improved for developing countries, and is likely, therefore, to support any international initiatives which have this in view. She has refused to join the low tariff club, GATT (General Agreement on Tariffs and Trade) since she wishes to preserve her own high tariffs. But she is an enthusiastic participant in the Latin American Free Trade Association, in the hope that she may be able to use this organization to open up the less developed countries of Latin America for her industrial goods.

RELATIONS WITH THE USA

Texas, New Mexico and Upper California were once a part of Mexico. In 1848 US forces were in occupation in Mexico City. As recently as 1914 US marines landed in and controlled the port of Vera Cruz. Madero was overthrown by Huerta with the connivance of the US Ambassador to Mexico, Henry Lane Wilson. His namesake, President Wilson, played a leading part in overthrowing Huerta and ensuring the triumph of Venustiano Carranza. It is impossible for Mexicans to forget these things, but they are now recognized as being past history. The present-day relationship between Mexico and the USA is based on mutual respect and the recognition of shared interests, both political and economic. The USA cannot afford to have an unfriendly power as a next-door neighbour which might be used by an enemy for subversive activities; but this does not mean that Mexico has to support slavishly all US policies in the international field. Mexico's policy of non-alignment is designed precisely to preserve her independence from any kind of US tutelage, and this is fully accepted and recognized in Washington. The same goes for economics. Sixty per cent of Mexican trade (imports and exports) is with the USA and 74 per cent of all foreign investment made recently in Mexico came from that country.[5] But here again there is no question of tutelage. US economic imperialism in Mexico is as dead as the dodo. American citizens who do business with Mexico do it on Mexican terms. Mexican credit is so good that she does not have to go hat in hand asking for gifts or loans; the international lending agencies are only too happy to let her have all the money she needs.

The turning-point in Mexican–US relations came when President Roosevelt gave his tacit support to Cárdenas on the issue of the oil expropriation. They were clinched when President Avila Camacho entered into a close alliance with the USA during World War 2. Since that time the two countries have never looked back. To quote Cline:[6]

From the occasion of the personal meeting of Presidents Roosevelt and Avila Camacho, to discuss mutual co-operation for the Second World War, an institutionalized ritual has been established wherein the new President of either country, Mexico or the United States, is invited to the other, partly as a symbolic affirmation of continuing cordiality and willingness to let bygones be bygones, partly to clear up any potential difficulties before they become serious. The decisions and agreements reached at these 'little summits' cover a wide range from plans for co-operative development of hydro-electric and irrigation projects along the Río Grande, to problems of credit, commodity prices, scientific co-operation in public health, malaria control, narcotics control, migrant labour. From these visits have often come unexpected small gestures that reveal the sincere attempts by leaders of each country to remove barriers to understanding and bury the past: President Truman's spontaneous placing of a wreath on the monument to the Boy Heroes [Cadets in the war of 1848 who wrapped themselves in Mexican flags and leaped to their deaths rather than surrender Mexico City] evoked an almost hysterical wave of favourable public emotion in Mexico.[7]

There are still some sore spots, of course. You do not have to scratch a Mexican very deeply to bring to the surface his latent fear and distrust of the *gringo*, coupled with contempt for the Anglo-Saxon culture which is considered crude when compared with that of the Latin world. There is constant pressure, too, from the left wing in Mexican politics for greater independence in Mexican foreign policy and more especially a tougher line on such issues as the treatment and status of Mexican migratory workers (the so-called *braceros*, who used to go in large numbers to the USA each year), or the damage being caused to Mexican crops by the high salt content of the irrigation water supplied by the Colorado River. But these are minor irritants. As in their financial policies, so too in their diplomacy the Mexicans show great prudence. They know which side their bread is buttered, but, if provoked, they will defend the national dignity to the last drop of their blood.

THE ORGANIZATION OF AMERICAN STATES

Mexico is a founder member of the Organization of American States, set up in 1948 as a successor to the Pan American Union which had been created in 1890. In its early days this inter-American organization was very largely dominated by the USA, especially in Central America and the Caribbean where US imperialism was rampant. Mexico found herself in the front line as the guardian of the frontier separating the Anglo-Saxon and Latin-American worlds. Hence her preoccupation with the doctrine of non-intervention, designed to prevent, apart from any further aggressions in Mexico, a recurrence of such US interventions in the affairs of Latin America as the occupation of the Dominican Republic (1916–24), Haiti (1915–34), Nicaragua (1912–24), and the various US incursions into Cuba (1906, 1912, 1917 and 1923). According to the so-called Estrada doctrine (formulated by a former Mexican Foreign Minister, Genaro Estrada) it is a cardinal principle of Mexican foreign policy to continue or discontinue her relations with other governments in accordance with Mexico's national interest, regardless of the way the other governments have come to power, the ideology to which they subscribe, or their domestic policies. This is, incidentally, the policy to which traditionally the United Kingdom has adhered in according diplomatic recognition to other powers. In both the Mexican and British views, a country should not use moral judgements about events in other countries as a pretext for intervention. It is, of course, a principle of particular importance in Latin America where so many governments, whether of the right or the left, came into power by a military coup d'état.

Mexico's policy of non-intervention was put to its sternest test at the Conference at Punta Del Este in January 1962 which suspended the present Cuban regime from membership in the Organization of American States. The USA, in fear of the spread of international communism in Latin America, were determined to clip the wings of Castro. Mexico ran a serious risk of prejudicing her relations with her powerful northern neighbour by not going along with the majority of Latin American States which supported the US position. But she stood firm by her principles. She based her case on the legal argument that there was no provision in the OAS charter for either expelling or suspending a member. But the Mexican delegation prudently stopped short of supporting the Argentine and Brazilian position, which in effect maintained that the controversy was between the USA and Cuba, and therefore the OAS and its other members were not involved – an unfriendly line which may possibly have been a contributory cause of the subsequent downfall of Frondizi and Goulart in their respective countries, while Mexico's close relations and friendship with the USA suffered no impairment.[8] This was a difficult moral decision for the Mexican Government to take, and she was fortunate in finding a legal loophole in the charter of the OAS. For on the left wing of Mexican politics, among the followers of Cárdenas, there were strong feelings in support of Castro who was regarded, not as a communist, but as a national revolutionary leader who was merely trying to do the same for Cuba as Mexico had done for herself fifty years before. So the Mexican Government found itself walking on a tight-rope. It has kept its balance by maintaining diplomatic relations with Castro, but at the same time keeping the relationship cool. Travellers to Cuba by air are carefully checked by the Mexican Security authorities (who have close links with the US security agencies), and measures have been taken to prevent Cuban propaganda entering Mexico by this route.

More generally, Mexico is a firm supporter of the underlying philosophy of the Alliance for Progress, which came into being in 1961 on the initiative of President John F. Kennedy. At this earlier meeting at Punta Del Este the Latin American republics committed themselves to a revolutionary programme of social and economic reform – comprehensive agrarian reform, fair wages and satisfactory working conditions, illiteracy to be wiped out, tax laws reformed, etc. The USA agreed to make available a major part of the minimum of 20 billion dollars needed to make the programme possible. In effect Kennedy was offering to underwrite a social revolution in Latin America on 'new frontier' lines. Mexico, with her own Revolution to serve as an example for more socially backward Latin American States, is in the best possible position to help and advise the USA in the promotion of this ambitious plan, which in spite of generous American aid, seems to have got bogged down in recent years. This is not surprising; for as this study should have brought out clearly, the social ills of Latin America, even in a relatively advanced country like Mexico, are deep-seated. It will probably take several generations before they can be cured, if indeed they can ever be entirely eradicated.

The OAS provides the formal framework for inter-American relationships. But Pan-Americanism, under the looming shadow of the USA, has not proved to be the best institutional framework for the creation of the political and economic integration of the countries of Latin America themselves, and there is now, accordingly, a tendency for these countries to draw together, both by closer bi-lateral relations and by creating purely Latin American bodies such as Lafta. The Mexican interest in the possibilities of economic integra-tion and wider inter-Latin American trade through Lafta has already been mentioned (p. 171). The visits to the Latin-American countries of President López Mateos (1958–64) – the first in history by a Mexican president – give proof of a new aim in Mexican foreign policy, de-signed to strengthen political and economic ties with the sister republics of Latin America.[9]

MEXICO IN THE UNITED NATIONS

Mexico is a founding member of the United Nations, which came into being at the San Francisco Conference in 1945. Of the fifty par-ticipating nations, no less than twenty were the republics of Latin America, giving them at the beginning a tremendous, and indeed inflated, influence in the affairs of the world organization. Even though, with the subsequent inclusion of so many new Asian and African countries, this forty per cent has been reduced to twenty, the Latin American votes may still be decisive in many committees. Not that the Latin American republics normally vote as a bloc. They hold regular informal meetings to discuss matters of common concern, but each country remains free to vote as it pleases on particular issues.

If non-intervention is the ruling principle of Mexican policy in the OAS, a policy of non-alignment is her guiding light in the UN. In Cold War issues Mexico will hold out a helping hand to the USA if her conscience allows her to do so, but she is quite prepared to support the Communist bloc on particular issues, and on a number of occasions has done so. Thus from 1947 to 1949 Mexico often abstained or was absent on votes relating to charges of Hungarian and Rumanian violations of provisions in the Balkan treaties protecting the rights of individuals and minorities. All other Latin American nations voted with the United States and against the Soviet Union on this issue. However, in the case of Soviet intervention in Hungary – a clear case of aggression – Mexico strongly supported the West. Similarly when Chinese Communists were fighting United Nations forces in Korea, Mexico regularly supported the United States in its refusal to consider the question of seating Communist China. But with the cessation of hostilities in Korea, Mexico has abstained on this question on a number of occasions. Mexico sided with the Soviet Union in supporting the admission of Albania, Hungary, Rumania, and Bulgaria to the United Nations in 1955, while the United States abstained.[10]

In view of the delicacy of her situation vis-à-vis the USA Mexico, according to Jorge Castañeda, prefers usually to place herself 'at a cautious distance from world problems'. She does not seek the lime-light. Thus, he points out, since 1946 Mexico has not participated in the work of the Security Council, although countries like Ecuador, Cuba, Brazil, Argentina and Colombia have been elected twice or even three times for periods of two years each. Even so, Mexico exerts an important influence and enjoys a high reputation in the United Nations. If she tries to keep clear of the major Cold War issues, on certain subjects, such as colonialism, disarmament and the problems of underdevelopment, in which she has a special interest, she has shown herself prepared to throw her weight about, voting on each issue as it comes up in accordance with her own views and without regard to their great power sponsorship. For example, with her own military establishment so small, Mexico has been energetic in seeking disarmament agreements with other Latin American countries, a policy which culminated in a recent treaty banning nuclear weapons in the region.

Thus, rather like Canada, Mexico is one of those rare members of the United Nations which judges each issue on its merits and votes accordingly. By following moderate policies and avoiding ideological stands on economic and political questions she sets a good example for all the nations, great and small. The United Nations would be a more useful body if there were more countries in it who followed a similar policy.

Mexico maintains direct diplomatic relations with most of the countries of the world. That with the USA is by far the most important of these relationships, followed, for political reasons, with those with her southern neighbours, Guatemala and Cuba. Outside the western hemisphere the importance of Mexico's bilateral relationships depend very largely upon the extent of trade, actual or potential.

A curious survival from the past, and one which seems at first sight to run counter to the principles of 'non-intervention' and 'non-alignment' is Mexico's lack of diplomatic relations with Franco's Spain. Among Mexicans generally there is still a good deal of affection for the mother country, and thousands of Mexican tourists spend holidays in Spain. The reason for the break in relations is historical. During the Spanish Civil War Mexico received with open arms a large number of Spanish republican refugees, many of whom have since become Mexican citizens. Under Cárdenas it was the official Mexican policy strongly to support the Spanish republican government in exile and recognize it as the legitimate government of Spain. This is still Mexico's position. Although the absence of Mexican relations with Franco makes little sense in modern ideological terms – many of the governments in Latin America are military dictatorships – it would cause a storm of left-wing criticism in Mexico if the policy towards Spain were reversed. For rather similar historical reasons Mexico does not maintain diplomatic relations with the Vatican.

Mexican relations with the countries behind the iron curtain are correct but cool; the two-way trade with this area is not significant. Because of alleged communist interference with the internal affairs of Mexico, relations with the USSR were broken in 1930, and were not renewed until 1942. Trotsky, who was a close friend of Diego Rivera, was given asylum in Mexico for three years until he was assassinated by Jacques Mornard on 20 August 1940. Today the threat of communist subversion is more likely to come from Cuba or China, and Mexican relations with the USSR have settled down into an uneventful routine.

In Mexico's pattern of trade with the world, the most significant development of recent times is a dropping off in the percentage of trade with the USA, which amounted to about 86 per cent in 1950, but is now down to about 60 per cent. This is a tendency which the Mexicans want to encourage, for it is not healthy for a country to have all its eggs in one basket. The Germans, the Japanese and the French have been the most active in picking up this business. The results of the British trade drive in Mexico have been disappointing, in spite of a visit by the British President of the Board of Trade in 1969. Britain's share of the Mexican market has been stuck at the meagre figure of $3\frac{1}{2}$–4 per cent during the last ten years; the Germans have been doing twice as well. A renewed British trade drive is in the making. The most pressing needs are for better credit arrangements and the appointment of more resident British representatives. There is plenty of potential business in Mexico for the enterprising British firm which is prepared to go and look for it.

Compared with the time of Porfirio Díaz, when the British stake in Mexico was second only to that of the USA, British influence in Mexico is now very small. But there is still a great deal of respect and good will for Britain to be found in Mexico. This good will has suffered some damage, however, in recent years, as the result of the spate of unfavourable and sometimes very unfair reports which appeared in the British press at the time of the Olympic Games and the World Cup. It is a great pity. Britain, as a leading if junior partner in the Atlantic Alliance, has a stake in the success of programmes such as the Alliance for Progress. No country in Latin America has done more than Mexico to bring about the kind of social revolution which it is the object of the Alliance to promote. Why not then give her a pat on the back, instead of denigrating her achievements?

A LAST WORD

In 1862, British, French and Spanish troops were landed in the port of Vera Cruz in order to collect unpaid debts, or as it was politely put at the time 'to offer a friendly hand to Mexico' and 'preside over her regeneration'. At this time Mexico was as poor as India, with 90 per cent of her people living in dire poverty, and the whole country in a chronic state of anarchy.

Today, a little more than a century later, the Mexican peso is a hard currency which has been used to support sterling. Mexico has emerged as one of the most stable and socially progressive countries of Latin America. In the front rank of the 'developing' countries of the world, Mexico is rapidly approaching, if she has not already achieved it, 'middle-power' status.

Thirty or forty years ago Mexico was still mainly a rural country, famed for its picturesque Indian peasantry. Foreigners used to go there 'to get away from it all' and they would return in raptures. Today the visitor is stunned by the size and bustle of Mexico City, and has to go quite far into the countryside before he finds any Indians. In a way perhaps the image of Mexico abroad has suffered as the consequence of such a rapid transformation. A really poor country with a colourful peasantry is accepted by the world for what it is, with compassion but without indignation. But Mexico has reached the awkward half-and-half stage in her development. With a surviving Indian peasantry on the one hand, and the modern aspect of the towns and the factories on the other, it is tempting to make invidious comparisons.

Taking for granted all that has been achieved the younger generation of Mexicans, and many foreign commentators on first acquaintance with the country, ask impatiently why the job has not been completed. All right, they concede grudgingly, Mexico may have distributed more land to the peasants than any other Latin American republic, but why are the peasants still poor? Mexico may have performed miracles in industrialization, but what is being done about the shanty-towns? Forty per cent of the people may have entered, or be about to enter, into the promised land of the middle class, but why do half the people still live in poverty? There may be many more schools and universities, but why is 20 per cent of the population still illiterate? Mexico may have evolved a political system, which has eliminated the military coup d'état and given the country forty years of stable and progressive government, but why not now give to the people the greater measure of democracy for which the young are clamouring?

It is my hope that this book will help to answer some of these questions, or at least put the problems in their proper perspective. All countries, whatever their place in the evolutionary scale, are faced by the daunting prospect of a mountain of unfinished business. Mexico is no exception. She is in the position of a mountaineer who, having successfully climbed one peak, now sees another equally high mountain lying in her path. There is a temptation to rest and enjoy the view, but this is impossible. She must press on. The next climb is going to be as arduous as the first, and it will take some time to reach the peak. But if past performance is any guide, there is no reason to suppose that it will not eventually be conquered.

Notes on the text

1 INTRODUCTION

1 Lesley Byrd Simpson, *Many Mexicos* (Berkeley and Los Angeles, 1952).

2 TOUR D'HORIZON

1 Graham Hutton, *Mexican Images* (London, 1963), p. 26.
2 Not to be confused with the village of Tepoztlán in Morelos described later.
3 Graham Hutton, *op. cit.*, p. 56.
4 Baja California, Chihuahua, Coahuila, Durango, Nuevo Léon, Sinaloa, Sonora and Tamaulipas.
5 R. H. K. Marett, *An Eye-witness of Mexico* (London, 1939).
6 Irene Nicholson, *The X in Mexico* (London, 1965), p. 163.
7 Irene Nicholson, *op. cit.*, p. 163.
8 Report in the Mexican newspaper *Excelsior*, 4 February 1970.
9 Graham Hutton, *op. cit.*, p. 66.

3 THE INDIAN HERITAGE

1 Octavio Paz, *The Labyrinth of Solitude*, translated by Lysander Kemp (New York, 1961), p. 32.
2 For a useful summary see Michael D. Coe, *Mexico* (Thames and Hudson).
3 The magnificent ruins of this city are within easy reach by car from the capital (see R. H. K. Marett, *Archaeological tours from Mexico City* (Mexico, 1964).
4 William H. Prescott, *The History of the Conquest of Mexico* (London, 1870).
5 Howard F. Cline, *Mexico: Revolution to Evolution* (London, 1962).
6 For example, the famous shrine of the Virgin of Guadalupe is built on the site of an older pagan shrine of the Earth Mother Goddess.

1　See, for example, Salvador de Madariaga, *The Rise and Fall of the Spanish American Empire* (London and New York, 1947), 2 vols.
2　Bernal Díaz de Castillo, *The Discovery and Conquest of Mexico* (London, 1928).
3　This famous Ahuehuete tree is still shown to tourists in Mexico City's suburb of Tacuba.
4　Charles Gibson, *Spain in America* (New York, 1966), p. 63.
5　Under the Spanish-colonial law each village was allotted a communal plot of land (*ejido*) which was supposed to be inalienable. Within the *ejido* each peasant family had the usufrucht of its own plot.
6　Gachupin was originally a derogatory term in Mexico. According to one interpretation it meant 'a wearer of spurs'; according to another 'a green-horn'.

1　In the following year Iturbide, attempting a come-back, was captured shortly after landing in Mexico, and executed.
2　Charles C. Cumberland, *Mexico – the Struggle for Modernity* (London, 1968), p. 141.
3　It is still debatable whether, in his negociations with President Polk, and later with General Scott, Santa Anna was trying to trick the enemy, or was ready to betray his country for his own personal ends.
4　Maximilian had signed his own death warrant when, in October 1865, he signed a decree instructing his troops to shoot all prisoners.

1　Ernest Gruening, *Mexico and its Heritage* (New York, 1928), p. 59.
2　The value of many of the schools was slight, partly because the teachers were miserably underpaid, partly because the children were often half-starved. (See H. B. Parkes, *A History of Mexico* (London, 1939), p. 302).
3　Later, alas, this railway fell upon evil days, with the opening of the Panama Canal. The service across the Isthmus was reduced to one train a day; and the fine harbour of Salina Cruz was allowed to silt up, until for a number of years a sand-bank completely blocked its entrance.
4　For more detail on this subject, see Charles C. Cumberland, *Mexico, the Struggle for Modernity* (London, 1968), chapter 8.

1　Calvert, *The Mexican Revolution 1910–1914: The Diplomacy of Anglo-American Conflict* (Cambridge, 1968), p. 42.

2 Madero's brother, Gustavo, was also murdered.
3 Subsequently the Commander-in-Chief of the US forces in France during the First World War.
4 The situation was graphically described in Graham Greene's novel *The Power and the Glory* (London, 1940).
5 At one point a compromise agreement was very nearly reached. But the companies upset Cárdenas by refusing to accept his verbal assurance on an important point. It will be recalled that the Americans made the same psychological error when negotiating with Obregón.

8 SOCIETY IN TRANSITION

1 Figure quoted by Cline, *The United States and Mexico* (Cambridge, Mass., 1963).
2 Figures quoted by Banco de Londres y Mexico, SA, in anniversary brochure 1864–1969.
3 See, for example, Whetton, *Rural Mexico*; Senior, *Land Reform and Democracy*; Eckstein, *The Collective Ejido*.
4 For detailed statistics, see Cline, *Mexico, Revolution to Evolution* (London, 1962), pp. 216-221.
5 Irene Nicholson, *The X in Mexico* (London, 1965), pp. 98-102.
6 Oscar Lewis, *Tepoztlán, village in Mexico* (Stanford, California, 1959).
7 David J. Scott, *Urbanization and Economic Development in Mexico* (London, 1969).
8 Oscar Lewis, *The Children of Sanchez* (USA, 1961).
9 Cline, *Mexico, Revolution to Evolution* (London, 1962), p. 125.
10 The statistics quoted were published by the Foreign Information Service of the First National City Bank, 1969.

9 THE PEOPLE AND POLITICS

1 The Government is able to exert pressure on the press through its control of the supply of newsprint.
2 *Sunday Times*, 4 June 1970.
3 That is why the PRI reacted so strongly when it looked in 1969 as though a rival party, PAN, might obtain control of Yucatan.
4 In the last Chamber of Deputies (August 1969) the PRI held 172 of the seats; 36 of the seats were occupied by members of the three opposition parties.
5 For a detailed and authoritative account of the Mexican political system see Frank Brandenburg, *The Makings of Modern Mexico* (New Jersey, 1964).
6 Illiteracy is now down to about 20 per cent of the population.

7 The peasants and workers have not so far shown any interest in the political activities of the students. But in the slums and lower ranks of the unions and peasant organizations there must be a good deal of inflammable material, which could be exploited.

8 This opinion was expressed to me by a highly-placed Mexican of left-of-centre views.

9 Under the direction of Dr Arthur Liebman (findings published in Excelsior, February 1970).

10 THE INTELLECTUAL AND SOCIAL CLIMATE

1 Quoted, Stephen Clissold, *Latin America – a Cultural Outline* (London, 1965).

2 Mexico has a flourishing films industry, and three outstanding stars in Dolores del Rio, Maria Felix and Mario Moreno (Cantinflas).

3 Victor Alba, *The Mexicans* (London, 1967).

4 Stephen Clissold, *op. cit.*

5 Cline, *Mexico: Revolution to Evolution* (London, 1962), pp. 128–129.

6 Graham Hutton, *Mexican Images* (London, 1963).

7 Quoted by Irene Nicholson, *The X in Mexico* (London, 1965), pp. 121–122.

8 It is located a few blocks away from the junction of Paseo de la Reforma and Avenida Insurgentes.

9 Oscar Lewis, *The Children of Sánchez* (USA, 1961).

10 In the altitude of Mexico City it is wise to eat a light supper at night.

11 MEXICO IN THE MODERN WORLD

1 Brazil, Argentina and Mexico.

2 Victor L. Urquidi, *The Challenge of Development in Latin America* (New York, 1964).

3 The US owned IPC, a subsidiary of Standard Oil of New Jersey.

4 See R. H. K. Marett, *Peru* (1969), pp. 263–264.

5 *Latin American International Politics*, edited by Carlos Alberto Astiz (Notre Dame, Indiana, 1969), p. 83.

6 Cline, *Mexico, Revolution to Evolution* (London, 1962), p. 305.

7 The most recent meeting in this series took place on 21 August 1970 in Puerto Vallarta during which Presidents Gustavo Días Ordaz and Richard M. Nixon discussed a treaty to settle several boundary disputes. Besides apportioning tracts of land in the Presidio valley and 320 islands in the Rio Grande, the agreement envisages maritime demarcations in the Gulf of Mexico and the Pacific Ocean and includes provisions for resolving future disputes. The problem of the Colorado River was also discussed.

8   *Latin American International Politics, op. cit.,* pp. 83-84.

9   Articles by Jorge Castaneda, in *Latin American International Politics, op. cit.*

10 Article by John R. Faust and Charles L. Stanifer in *Latin American International Politics, op. cit.*

Acknowledgments

American Museum of Natural History, 1; Associated Press, 28; Camera Press, 8, 9, 24, 27; Editorial Fund for Mexican Plastic Arts, 17; Irmgard Groth-Kimball, 3; Stephen Harrison, 20; Mexican National Tourist Council, 5, 19, 22, 23, 25, 26; Organization of American States, 4, 21 (Betty and Arthur Reef), 30 (Hamilton Wright); Radio Times Hulton Picture Library, 7, 10, 11, 12, 13, 14, 15, 16; Staatliche Museen zu Berlin, 6; United Press International, 29; University of Pennsylvania Museum, 18.

Select bibliography

(limited to works in English)

GENERAL HISTORIES

Cumberland, Charles C., *Mexico: the Struggle for Modernity*, London, 1968

McHenry, J. Patrick, *A Short History of Mexico*, New York, 1962

Parkes, H. B., *A History of Mexico*, Cambridge, Mass., 1938

INDIAN CIVILIZATIONS

(There is a large technical literature; the following are some useful modern surveys)

Coe, Michael D., *Mexico*, London, 1962; *The Maya*, London, 1966

Marett, Sir Robert, *Archaeological Tours from Mexico City*, Mexico City, 1964

Morley, Sylvanus G., *The Ancient Maya*, Stanford, 1946

Soustelle, Jacques, *The Daily Life of the Aztecs*, London, 1961

Thompson, J. E. S., *The Rise and Fall of Maya Civilization*, Oklahoma, 1954; *Mexico Before Cortés*, New York, 1933

Vaillant, George C., *Aztecs of Mexico*, New York, 1962

INDIAN FOLK-LORE

Covarrubias, Miguel, *Mexico South*, London, 1947

Fergusson, Erna, *Fiesta in Mexico*, New York, 1934

Gallop, Rodney, *Mexican Mosaic*, London, 1939

Toor, Frances, *A Treasury of Mexican Folkways*, New York, 1947

SPANISH CONQUEST

Cortés, Hernando, *Five Letters, 1519–1526*, London, 1928

Díaz Del Castillo, Bernal, *The Discovery and Conquest of Mexico, 1517–1521*, London, 1928

Innes, Hammond, *The Conquistadores*, London, 1969

Prescott, William H., *History of the Conquest of Mexico*, London, 1870

187

COLONIAL PERIOD
(See also General Histories. The following books deal exclusively with this period)

Haring, C. H., *The Spanish Empire in America*, New York, 1947

Madariaga, Salvador de, *The Rise and Fall of the Spanish American Empire*, London and New York, 1942, 2 vols.

Parry, J. H., *The Spanish Seaborne Empire*, London and New York, 1966

THE MEXICAN REPUBLIC (to 1910)
(See also General Histories; the following books are recommended for supplementary reading)

Beals, Carlton, *Porfirio Díaz*, Philadelphia and London, 1932

Calderon de la Barca, Mme, *Life in Mexico*, London, 1843

Callcott, W. H., *Santa Anna*, Oklahoma, 1936

Corti, Egon, Count, *Maximilian and Charlotte of Mexico*, London, 1928

Flandrau, C. M., *Viva Mexico*, London, 1908

Roeder, Ralph, *Juárez and his Mexico*, New York, 1947

Young, Desmond, *Member for Mexico* (a biography of Weetman Pearson, First Viscount Cowdray), London, 1966

THE MEXICAN REVOLUTION (1911–1940)

Atkin, Ronald, *Revolution! Mexico 1910–1920*, Bristol, 1969

Calvert, Peter, *The Mexican Revolution 1910–1914: the Diplomacy of Anglo-American Conflict*, Cambridge, 1968

Dulles, John W. F., *Yesterday in Mexico: a chronicle of the Revolution, 1919–1936*, Austin, Texas, 1961

Evans, Rosalie, *Letters from Mexico*, New York, 1926

Gruening, Ernest, *Mexico and its Heritage*, New York, 1928

King, Rosa, *Tempest over Mexico*, New York and London, 1928

Kirk, Betty, *Covering the Mexican Front*, Oklahoma, 1942

Marett, R. H. K., *An Eye-witness of Mexico*, London, 1939

McCullagh, Captain Francis, *Red Mexico*, New York and London, 1928

O'Shaughnessy, Edith, *A Diplomat's Wife in Mexico*, New York, 1916

Reed, John, *Insurgent Mexico*, New York and London, 1914

Simpson, Eyler N., *The Ejido, Mexico's Way Out*, Chapel Hill, North Carolina, 1937

Tannenbaum, Frank, *Peace by Revolution*, New York, 1933

Waugh, Evelyn, *Robbery under Law*, London, 1939

Weyl, Nathaniel and Sylvia, *The Reconquest of Mexico: the years of Lázaro Cárdenas*, Oxford, 1939

Womack, John, Jr., *Zapata and the Mexican Revolution*, London, 1969

CONTEMPORARY MEXICO
Alba, Victor, *The Mexicans*, London, 1967
Brandenburg, Frank, *The Makings of Modern Mexico*, New Jersey, 1964
Cline, Howard F., *Mexico: Revolution to Evolution*, London, 1962; *The United States and Mexico*, Cambridge, Mass., 1961
Hutton, Graham, *Mexican Images*, London, 1963
Nicholson, Irene, *The X in Mexico*, London, 1965
Padgett, L. Vincent, *The Mexican Political System*, Boston, Mass., 1966

SOCIOLOGICAL STUDIES
Lewis, Oscar, *The Children of Sánchez*, Harmondsworth, 1961; *Pedro Martinez*, London, 1964; *Tepoztlan, Village in Mexico*, Stanford, Cal., 1959
Redfield, Robert, *Tepoztlan: a Mexican Village*, Chicago, 1930

IMPRESSIONS OF MEXICO
Greene, Graham, *The Lawless Roads*, London, 1939
Huxley, Aldous, *Beyond the Mexique Bay*, Harmondsworth, 1955
Lawrence, D. H., *Mornings in Mexico*, Harmondsworth, 1956; *The Plumed Serpent*, Harmondsworth, 1955
Spratling, William, *Little Mexico*, New York, 1932
Wright, Norman Pelham, *Mexican Kaleidoscope*, London, 1947; *Mexican Medley for the Curious*, Mexico City, 1961

LITERATURE
Azuela, Mariano, *The Trials of a Respectable Family* and *The Underdogs* (published in one volume), San Antonio, Texas, 1963
Fuentes, Carlos, *The Death of Artemio Cruz*, New York, 1964
Greene, Graham, *The Power and the Glory*, London, 1940
Guzman, Martin Luis, *The Eagle and the Serpent* (translated), New York, 1930
Paz, Octavio, *The Labyrinth of Solitude; Life and Thought in Mexico*, London, 1961

ART AND ARCHITECTURE
Baird, J. A., Jnr., *The Churches of Mexico, 1530–1810*, California, 1962
Joyce, T. A., *Maya and Mexican Art,* London, 1926
Kubler, George, *The Art and Architecture of Ancient America*, Harmondsworth, 1962
Plenn, Virginia and Jaime, *A Guide to Modern Mexican Murals*, Mexico City, 1963
Sanford, Trent E., *The Story of Architecture in Mexico*, New York, 1947

Who's Who

ALAMÁN, Lucas (1792–1853). Nineteenth-century historian and intellectual leader of the Conservative Party. In the last year of his life he served as a Minister under the Dictator, Santa Anna, whom he had been largely instrumental in bringing back to power.

ALEMÁN, Miguel (b. 1902). Appointed Governor of Vera Cruz in 1936, he moved to the national scene as campaign manager and Minister of Government (Interior) for President Avila Camacho. As President of Mexico (1946–52) he was the author of a programme of massive economic development. He is currently (1970) Head of the Mexican Tourist Bureau, and wields great influence on the right wing of the PRI.

AZUELA, Mariano (1873–1952). A physician by profession, he became the first of the revolutionary novelists. His most famous book, *Los de Abajo* (The Under-dogs) was published in 1916.

CALLES, Plutarco Elías (1877–1945). A small-town schoolmaster in Sonora and revolutionary general, he was President of Mexico 1924–28, and subsequently ruled behind the scenes as a virtual dictator until forced into exile by President Cárdenas in 1936. Beginning his political career as a radical, and stamping fiercely upon the Roman Catholic Church, he became increasingly conservative during his last years of power, and did a great deal to promote economic development. He was one of the principal founders of the revolutionary Party (PNR), now become the PRI.

CAMACHO, Manuel Avila (1897–1955). Revolutionary general and Minister of War under President Cárdenas, he succeeded the latter as President 1940–46. A moderate in politics, he inaugurated a period of 'consolidation'. Bringing Mexico into the war on the side of the Allies, he concerted a close alliance with the USA, to the great benefit of the Mexican economy.

CÁRDENAS, Lázaro (1895–1970). Revolutionary general and former Governor of Michoacán, he was President of Mexico 1934–40. In defiance of Calles, whom he forced into exile, Cárdenas gave Mexico the strongest dose of revolutionary government it has ever experienced, pushing ahead vigorously with agrarian reform, strongly supporting the labour unions and expropriating the foreign-controlled oil industry. Regarded as the Grand Old Man of the Revolution, he exerted great influence on the left wing of the PRI.

CARRANZA, Venustiano (1859–1920). Landowner and Senator during the time of Porfirio Díaz and a former Governor of Coahuila, he supported the revolution of Francisco Madero in 1911. After the latter's death he led the revolt against Victoriano Huerta, assuming the title of First Chief of the Constitutionalist Army. Victorious over his rivals in the revolutionary movement, he occupied the presidency 1915–20, during which time the famous Constitution of 1917 was promulgated. Overthrown by a military revolt, he was assassinated in 1920.

CASO, Alfonso (b. 1896). Mexico's leading anthropologist and archeologist, he excavated the ruins of Monte Alban, discovering a rich hoard of Zapotec gold. He was appointed Director of the Indigenous Institute in 1949.

CASO, Antonio (1883–1946). Elder brother of Alfonso; one of Mexico's most eminent philosophers in the first half of the twentieth century.

CORTÉS, Hernan (1485–1547). The intrepid leader of the Spanish expedition to Mexico. Created a Marquis, he was the first Governor of the colony (1522–26), but returned to Spain under a cloud and died a disappointed man.

CUAUHTÉMOC (d. 1524). The last Emperor of the Aztecs (1520–22), he conducted the gallant last-ditch defence of Tenochtitlan. He was captured and tortured by the Spaniards, and executed in 1524.

DÍAZ, Porfirio (1830–1915). Born in Oaxaca of humble parentage, he made his name as a general in the army of the Liberal Reform movement. Having quarrelled with Juarez, against whom he led an abortive revolt in 1871, he managed to seize power in 1876 and thenceforth ruled Mexico as a dictator (with one short interlude) until overthrown in 1911. He died in exile in 1915. Díaz gave Mexico thirty-five years of law, order and financial stability and laid some of the foundations for the country's subsequent industrial progress. But these benefits were obtained at the cost of political and social oppression.

DÍAZ, Felix. Nephew of Porfirio Díaz. In alliance with Huerta he led the the revolt which unseated Madero in 1913. But although he had been promised the post by Huerta, the latter clung to the presidency, and Díaz was disappointed in his ambition to follow in the footsteps of his illustrious uncle.

DÍAZ ORDAZ, Gustavo (b. 1911). A native of Puebla, and Minister of Interior during the presidency of Lopez Mateos, he was President of Mexico 1964–70. He pushed forward vigorously with agrarian reform and economic development. His most troublesome problem was student unrest, which came to a head very awkwardly for his government just before the Olympic Games in 1968.

ECHEVERRÍA, Luis (b. 1922). Having occupied various posts in the PRI since 1946, he became Minister of Interior under Díaz Ordaz, and was selected by the Party to be the presidential candidate in 1970. He won the election with 84% of the total vote. He has promised that his top priority will be the problems of the peasantry.

FARÍAS, Valentín Gómez (1781–1858). A physician from Zacatecas who for a quarter of a century was recognized as the leader of the Liberal Party. He was acting President 1833–39, but was deposed by Santa Anna, who disapproved of his reforming zeal. He occupied the presidency again in 1847 only to be ousted a second time by Santa Anna. As an old man he was carried into the hall on a litter in order to be the first to pledge allegiance to the Liberal Constitution of 1857.

FUENTES, Carlos (b. 1929). One of the most outstanding of the younger generation of Mexican writers. Among his best-known works are *La Región Más Transparente* (1958), commenting critically on post-revolutionary Mexican society, and *La Muerte de Artemio Cruz* (1962), telling the story of a revolutionary general.

GUADALUPE VICTORIA (1789–1843). Born with the name Felix Fernandez, a native of Durango and a law student, he fought as a guerrilla chieftain during the War of Independence. He was the first President of the Mexican Republic 1824–29.

GUERRERO, Vicente (1783–1831). Son of a peasant, he joined the independence movement in the army of Morelos; after the death of the latter he held out as a guerrilla leader in the mountains of the State which bears his name. His pact with Iturbide, known as the Plan of Iguala, led to the independence of Mexico. President of the Republic in 1829, he was deposed in the following year and executed.

GUZMAN, Martin Luis (b. 1887). Revolutionary writer. In his most famous novel, *The Eagle and the Serpent*, he uses Pancho Villa, who was a close friend, as the model for the hero.

HIDALGO Y COSTILLO, Miguel (1753–1811). Parish priest of the town of Dolores, he initiated the movement towards independence with his famous *Grito de Dolores* (16 September, 1810). A humanitarian with sympathy for the oppressed Indians, he suddenly found himself in command of a revolutionary army which he could not control, and a massacre of Spaniards followed. Excommunicated by the Church, he was captured and executed in 1811. He is now regarded as a national hero.

HUERTA, Adolfo de la. One of the triumvirate of revolutionary politicians from Sonora which overthrew Carranza in 1920. He was named Provisional President pending the election of Obregón. When, in 1924, Calles was selected to succeed Obregón, de la Huerta organized an unsuccessful revolt. In exile in Los Angeles he became an opera singer.

HUERTA, Victoriano (1845–1916). A leading general in the army of Madero, he betrayed his master and succeeded him as President of Mexico in 1913. Tough, unscrupulous and an alcoholic, Huerta was supported by the conservatives and foreign capital. But although he was recognized by Britain, President Woodrow Wilson refused to recognize Huerta's government and supplied arms to the revolutionary armies in the north under Carranza. Defeated by Carranza, Huerta departed into exile in 1914.

ITURBIDE, Agustín (1783–1824). A Creole soldier of fortune, he was ordered by the Spanish Viceroy to hunt down the elusive guerrilla leader Vicente Guerrero. Instead he entered into a pact with Guerrero and, in his Plan of Iguala (1821), proclaimed the independence of Mexico. Being named 'emperor' in 1822, his imperial glory was short-lived and he was forced to abdicate in 1823, retiring into exile. Attempting a come-back in the following year, he was captured when landing on the coast and shot.

JUÁREZ, Benito (1806–72). A pure-blooded Zapotec Indian, he studied for the priesthood but entered the law instead and was appointed Governor of his native State of Oaxaca. Minister of Justice in the liberal governments of Alvarez and Comonfort, he decreed the abolition of clerical and military *fueros* (Ley Juárez, 1855). After the defection of Comonfort in 1858, Juárez assumed leadership of the Liberal Party and was proclaimed President in Querétaro, but it was only after three years of civil war that he was able to enter the capital in 1861. There followed the French intervention and the imposition of Maximilian as emperor, but Juárez steadfastly refused to yield to the foreign usurper and Maximilian was captured and shot in 1867. Thereafter Juárez ruled more or less peacefully as the first civilian President of Mexico until struck down by a heart attack in 1872. A man of great integrity and ability, he occupies an honoured place in Mexican history.

LERDO DE TEJADA, Miguel (1812–61). Secretary of the Treasury in the liberal government of Comonfort, he drafted the controversial *Ley Lerdo* which laid down, *inter alia*, that all the estates owned by the Church were to be sold. He served later in the cabinet of Juárez during the civil war. In 1861 he announced his candidature for the presidency, but died a month before the election took place, and Juárez was re-elected.

LERDO DE TEJADA, Sebastian (1827–89). Brother of Miguel and another distinguished liberal. For eight years the inseparable associate of Juárez, Lerdo stood unsuccessfully as a presidential candidate in 1871 against his old master who was re-elected for a fourth term. Lerdo became President of the Supreme Court, succeeding to the presidency in the following year upon the death of Juárez. He was overthrown by Porfirio Díaz in 1876 when he announced that he proposed to seek re-election for a second term.

LIMANTOUR, José Ives. The son of a French adventurer who had dug for gold in California and later acquired land in Mexico, he was a leading spirit in the small clique of *científicos* who surrounded Porfirio Díaz in his later years. Made Secretary of the Treasury in 1893, he balanced the budget and laid the economic foundations of the remarkable economic prosperity of the Porfirian epoch. He acquired for Mexico control over most of the railroads. A potential successor to Porfirio Díaz, he conducted peace negotiations with Francisco Madero in 1911 which resulted in the overthrow of Díaz. A week later he followed Díaz into exile.

LOMBARDO TOLEDANO, Vicente (1894–1968). Left-wing labour leader and intellectual, he led the revolt within the CROM against the domination of Luis Morones (see below). He was appointed Secretary of the Confederación de Trabajadores de Mexico (CTM) when this new confederation was formed in 1936. A powerful and controversial figure in Mexican politics, he was eased out of the CTM by President Alemán, because of his Communist leanings. He then formed his extreme left-wing Partido Popular Socialista, which has continued in being since his death in 1968, but has little influence.

LÓPEZ MATEOS, Adolfo (b. 1910). A lawyer and professor by background, he became Secretary-General of the PRI and served as Minister of Labour in the government of Ruiz Cortinez. President of Mexico 1958–64, he pushed forward vigorously with agrarian reform and economic development and took an active interest in foreign affairs. He opposed the resolutions sponsored by Washington for ousting Castro's Cuba from the OAS, but condemned the presence of communism in the American continent. He held frequent meetings with Eisenhower, Kennedy and Lyndon Johnson and succeeded in settling the dispute with the USA over the Chamizal territory. He developed closer links between Mexico and the Latin American republics, and the new countries of Asia and Africa.

MADERO, Francisco (1873–1913). Descended from a wealthy family in Coahuila, he was educated in France and the USA, where he picked up humanitarian ideas. A dedicated and idealistic liberal, he published in 1908 a book proclaiming the need for political freedom, while accepting the re-election of Díaz. Ignored by Díaz, he announced his candidature for the presidency in 1910, but was imprisoned just before the elections took place. Released after the re-election of Díaz, he published in 1911 his *Plan of San Luis Potosí* calling for the overthrow of the dictator. The Mexican Revolution was thus launched, and he became President 1911–13. Not strong enough to control the revolutionary forces he had unleashed, he was overthrown by Huerta and Feliz Díaz and brutally assassinated by his guards. Criticized by both friends and foes during his lifetime, he is now revered as a martyr of the Mexican Revolution.

MAXIMILIAN (1832–67). Younger brother of the Hapsburg Emperor of Austria, this unfortunate Archduke was induced by Napoleon III to become the Emperor of Mexico (1864) and was placed on his rickety throne by a French expeditionary force. He disappointed his conservative and clerical backers by refusing to restore the Church lands, while the liberals under Juárez engaged in a relentless guerrilla war against the usurpers. Deserted by Napoleon, who withdrew the French forces (his wife Carlotta went mad in the Vatican while appealing for help to the Pope), Maximilian's Mexican army was defeated by the liberals at Querétaro. The Emperor and two of his principal generals were shot.

MOCTEZUMA (d. 1520). Ruler of the Aztec empire from 1502 to 1522. As a prisoner of Cortés he continued in nominal charge of the empire until stoned to death by his own people when they revolted against the Spaniards.

MORELOS, José María (1765–1815). Parish priest of Caracuaro in Michoacán, he joined the revolutionary army of Hidalgo with twenty-five followers; before the end of 1811 he commanded an army of nine thousand men and controlled a large part of western Mexico. After the death of Hidalgo he became the leader of the independence movement. At a Congress at Chilpancingo over which he presided in 1813 far-reaching proposals for social and agrarian reform were put forward. But his army was defeated by the Spaniards, and he was captured and shot in 1815.

MORONES, Luis. Mexico's first national labour leader. He organized six 'red battalions' of workers to fight on the side of Carranza, but was later imprisoned by the latter for his part in organizing strikes in 1916. Brought back into favour by President Obregón, he organized in 1918 a national federation of labour unions (CROM) which dominated the labour scene until superseded by the present-day CTM. Having become ostentatiously rich, while continuing as a labour leader, he was despatched into exile (together with Calles) by President Cárdenas in 1936.

OBREGÓN, Álvaro (1880–1928). Revolutionary general from Sonora, and right-hand man of Carranza. However, when the latter tried to impose on the country an unpopular successor, he revolted against his old master, and was elected President for the period 1920–24. By background a farmer, he took an interest in agrarian matters, supported the labour unions and promoted education. Chosen to succeed Calles as President for a second term, he was assassinated by a religious fanatic in 1928.

ORTIZ RUBIO, Pascual (1885–1963). An engineer by profession, he occupied the presidency 1930–32, while Calles ruled behind the scenes. When he showed some signs of independence in making cabinet appointments, he was forced by Calles to resign.

OROZCO, Jose Clemente (1883–1949). One of Mexico's big-three muralists of the revolutionary period. A tragic and dramatic artist, his monumental works reveal a profoundly human spirit and a fierce sense of identification with his times.

PAZ, Octavio (b. 1914). A well-known contemporary Mexican poet. His most famous work is *The Labyrinth of Solitude*, which was translated into English by Lysander Kemp in 1961.

PORTES GIL, Emilio (b. 1891). A radical lawyer and former Governor of Tamaulipas, he became Provisional President of Mexico in 1928 after the murder of Obregón, retaining the post until 1930. He was a co-founder with Calles of the official Party, PNR (now PRI). He was President of the PNR until removed by Cárdenas in 1936.

RIVERA, Diego (1886–1957). Having studied in Paris, he was the pioneer of the new Mexican revolutionary school of art. Drawing inspiration from both European and Maya and Aztec art, his vast frescoes in many of the public buildings of Mexico tell the story of the Mexican Revolution with the political passion of a convinced Marxist and the brush of a master.

RODRÍGUEZ, Abelardo b. 1889. Revolutionary general and wealthy business man (he owned two casinos among his many interests), he was chosen by Calles to succeed Ortiz Rubio as President, and ruled the country, under the shadow of Calles, from 1932 until 1934.

RUIZ CORTÍNES, Adolfo. A career civil servant, chosen by the PRI to succeed as President (1952–58) the dynamic Alemán; he inherited a good many problems. By slowing down the tempo of economic development he gave Mexico an indispensable breathing spell; in politics he steered a middle course between the policies of the supporters of Alemán and Cárdenas in the PRI.

SANTA ANNA, Antonio López de (1794–1876). A remarkable soldier-politician who dominated the political life of Mexico for thirty-five years in the early part of the nineteenth century (for the highlights of his stormy career, see pp. 73–5). He was first elected President in 1833, and thereafter (with intervening periods of retirement or exile) occupied the presidency in 1839, 1841–45, 1846–47, and 1853–55. He died, blind and penniless, in 1876.

SIERRA, Justo (1848–1912). Poet, essayist and intellectual giant during the time of Porfirio Díaz. As Minister of Education he established the new university and doubled the number of schools. His written works include *Evolución Politica del Pueblo Mexicano* (Political Evolution of the Mexican People) and *Juárez, Su Obra y Su Tiempo* (Juarez, his Work and Times).

SIQUEIROS, David Alfaro (b. 1898). Revolutionary painter and muralist. Because of alleged subversive activities on the extreme left wing of politics, he was jailed in 1960 (during which time he continued to paint) and released by special amnesty in July 1964.

VASCONCELOS, José (1881–1958). One of the original supporters of Madero, he was an energetic and dedicated Minister of Education under Obregón. He broke his links with the revolutionary movement after the failure of his candidature in the presidential election of 1929. Retiring to the USA, he devoted his remaining energies to writing. He must be rated as one of

Mexico's leading intellectuals, although the strongly hispanophile bias of his views is not to everybody's taste.

VILLA, Pancho (1877–1923). The most picturesque of the revolutionary leaders, this former ranch-hand (who became an outlaw after he had avenged the rape of his sister by the son of the landowner) organized an army in the north in support of Madero. After the murder of Madero (who once saved his life) he fought against Huerta and Carranza and in 1914 succeeded, together with Zapata, in occupying Mexico City. Driven out of the capital, he continued guerrilla warfare in the north until brought to heel by Obregón. In 1916 he raided the US town of Columbus, New Mexico, and Pershing was sent into Mexico but failed to capture him. He was assassinated by political enemies in 1923.

ZAPATA, Emiliano (1880–1919). Peasant leader of revolutionary forces in the southern States of Morelos, Guerrero and Puebla. He seized and demanded land for the peasants and withdrew his support for Madero when the latter failed to institute land reforms. With Villa, Zapata captured Mexico City in 1914 and fought tenaciously against Huerta and Carranza. Led into a trap by Guajardo, an officer in Carranza's army, he was assassinated in 1919. He is revered in Mexico as the father of agrarian reform.

Index

Numbers in italic refer to illustrations

ACAPULCO, 10, 18
agrarian reform, 98–9, 102, 103–4,
   106, 107, 108, 110, 113, 119,
   120, 131–6, 161, 170
agriculture, 13, 21, 24, 25, 30, 42,
   61–2, 89–91, 93
Aguascalientes Convention (1914),
   101
Águila y la Serpiente, El (Guzman),
   160
Agustín I, emperor, *see* Iturbide
Alamán, Lucas (*see* Who's Who,
   p. 191), 73
Alemán, Miguel (*see* Who's Who,
   p. 191), 118–19, 120, 132, 143,
   148, 152
Allende, Ignacio, 67, 68
Alliance for Progress, 174
Almazán, Gen. Juan Andreu, 118
Álvarez, Juan, 76
Anahuac, Vale of, *see* Valley of
   Mexico
anarchism, 158
anarcho-syndicalism, 93
Anthropological Museum, 164
Apra (Peruvian party), 170
archeological remains, 9, 10, 20,
   26, 29, 30
architecture, 10, 47, 49–50, 164

Argentine, 169, 174
Arista, Gen. Mariano, 75
army, 70, 71, 84, 113, 170
art, 10, 18, 47, 50, 52, 107, 159–60,
   164
Artes Populares en Mexico, Las
   (Atl), 160
Atl, Dr, 160
Aztec peoples and culture, 16, *33*,
   44–8 *passim*, 54–6, 135, 159
Azuela, Mariano (*see* Who's Who,
   p. 191), 160, 161

BALSAS VALLEY, 133
Barra, Francisco León de la, 97
Bassols, Narciso, 114
Bodet, Jaime Torres, 163
Bonillas, Ignacio, 106
Brazil, 169, 174
Bucareli, Antonio de, 66
Burgos, laws of, 57
Bustamante, Gen. Anastasio, 74

CABRERA, Luis, 99
California, 75, 87
Calleja, Gen. Félix, 68

Calles, Gen. Plutarco Elias (*see* Who's Who, p. 191), 107–11, 112, 131, 133, 148, 152, 153

Camacho, Gen. Avila (*see* Who's Who, p. 191), 117–18, 132, 152, 162, 172

Cananea mines, civil disorders at, 93

Cannabal, Garrido, 109

Carden, Sir Lionel, 101

Cárdenas, Gen. Lázaro (*see* Who's Who, p. 192), 111–18 *passim*, 120, 131, 148, 152, 154, 162, 172, 174

Carlotta, wife of Archduke Maximilian, 78, 79

Carranza, Venustiano (*see* Who's Who, p. 192), *38*, 101, 102–6 *passim*

Casa del Obrero Mundial, 103, 106, 110, 113

Casas, Bartolomé de las, 57

Caso, Dr Alfonso (*see* Who's Who, p. 192), 134

Caso, Antonio (*see* Who's Who, p. 192), 158

Castañeda, Jorge, 176

Castro, Fidel, 173, 174

cattle ranching, 24; by-products, 62

Cedillo, Gen. Saturnino, 117

Chapultepec Park, Museum of Modern Art, 164

Charles V, emperor, 56

Charles III of Spain, 66

chemical industry, 141, 143

Chichén Itzá, 30–1, *34*

Chichimec peoples, 44, 46, 47

Chihuahua, 90, 96, 99, 101, 141

Children of Sánchez, The (Lewis), 137–9

Chilpancingo, Congress of (1813), 68

Cholula, 19

'*Cientificos*', 92–3, 97, 159

Ciudad Obregón, 25

climate, 14–15

Cline, Howard F., 49, 172

CNC, *see* Confederation Nacional Campesina

Coahuila, 95, 101, 141

Coatzacoalcos, 27, 87

Columbus (New Mexico), 102

communications, 11, 17 *et seq.*, 28, 86–8, 142

communism, 159

communist bloc, Mexican relations with, 175–6, 177

Comonfort, Ignacio, 76, 77

Confederacion Nacional Campesina, 113, 148

conservatives, Mexican, 71, 77, 78, 79, 84, 154

Constitution (1857), 76–7, 146

Constitution (1917), 103–5, 107, 108, 115, 146–7, 153

Consulados merchant guilds, 62

Corral, Ramón, 96

Corregidores, 58, 59, 66

Cortés, Hernan (*see* Who's Who, p. 192), 16, *35*, 52, 53, 55, 56, 57, 58

cosmopolitanism of society, under Díaz, 92–3

cotton production, 24, 25, 95, 114, 133

Cowdray, First Viscount, 86–8, 97
crafts, 47, 50
Creoles, 63, 67, 68, 70, 71
'Cristo Rey' revolt, 108
CROM, 106, 110, 113
CTM, 112, 148
Cuatitlán, 142
Cuauhtémoc (*see* Who's Who, p. 192), 52
Cuba, 75, 173–4, 177
Cuernavaca, 17–18, 135, 142

Decena Tragica, 99–100
Díaz, Bernal, 55
Díaz, Carmen, 84
Díaz, Felix (*see* Who's Who, p. 193), 99
Díaz Ordaz, Gustavo (*see* Who's Who, p. 193), 120
Díaz, Porfirio (*see* Who's Who, p. 192), *38*, 82–96, 97, 102, 147, 161
Dominican Republic, 173
Dos Bocas oil well, 88
Durango, 141

ECHEVERRÍA, Luis (*see* Who's Who, p. 193), 27, *126*, 131, 133, 140, 146, 150, 151, 152, 154, 155, 157
economic growth, *see* industrialization
education, 84, 107, 152–3
Ejido, Mexico's Way Out, The (Simpson), 161
ejidos, 62, 104, 108, 113, 114, 131*ff*.

encomendero, 57–8
encomienda, 57–8, 61
Enlightenment, influence of, on Mexico, 66
epidemics, 61
Estrada, Genaro, 173

FAMILY LIFE, 165–6; *see also* Sánchez family
Farías, Valentín Gómez (*see* Who's Who, p. 193), 72–3, 74
fascism, 116, 162
Ferdinand VII, king of Spain, 67, 69
fiesta, 50–1, *128*
food, 50; *see also* agriculture
France, 78, 79
Franco, General, 116, 177
friars, 57, 60
Fuentes, Carlos (*see* Who's Who, p. 193), 162
fueros (immunities of Church and army), 72, 76

Gachupines, 63
Gálvez, José de, 66
GATT, 171
geography of Mexico, 13–31
Gómez, Francisco Vásquez, 97
González, Gen. Manuel, 85
governors, State, 150–2
Great Britain, interests in Mexico, 77–8, 85, 86, 88, 96, 98, 100, 101, 116, 117, 173, 178
Greene, Graham, 29
Gruening, Ernest, 161

Guadalajara, 21, 137, 142
Guadalupe Victoria (*see* Who's
 Who, p. 193), 69, 70, 73
Guatemala, 88, 177
Guerrero, Vicente (*see* Who's
 Who, p. 193), 69, 70, 73
Guerrero region, 26–7
Gutiérrez, Eulalio, 101
Guzman, Martin Luis (*see* Who's
 Who, p. 194), 160
haciendas, 61–2, 63, 64, 68, 71, 72,
 89, 90, 98, 104, 136

Haiti, 173
Hawaii, 87
Herrera, Gen. José Joaquin, 75
Herrera, Rudolfo, 106
Hidalgo y Costillo, Fr. Miguel (*see*
 Who's Who, p. 194), *36*, 66–8,
 72, 80
Hispanidad, concept of, 53–4
Houston, Sam, 74
Huerta, Adolfo de la (*see* Who's
 Who, p. 194), 106, 108
Huerta, Victoriano (*see* Who's
 Who, p. 194), 99, 100, 101, 103
hydro-electricity, 24, 27, 30, 142,
 172

INDEPENDENCE, Mexico's
 declaration of (1810), 66;
 achievement of, 69
Indian population, 25–6, 27–8, 30,
 41–52 *passim*, 64, 71, 72, 80, 83,
 85, 90, 92, 134–5, 159, 161, 163,
 179; colonial impositions on,
 59–60
Indigenous Institute, 134

Indio, El (Fuentes), 161
industrialization, 85–9 *passim*, 110,
 118, 119, 140–5, 161
Interoceanic Railway, 97
investment, foreign, 85–9 *passim*,
 93, 104, 107, 108, 109, 113,
 115–17, 119, 144, 158–9, 171
irrigation, 24–5, 90, 108, *123*, 132,
 133, 134, 172, 173
Iturbide, Agustín de (*see* Who's
 Who, p. 194–5), 69, 73
Iturrigary, José de, 67

Juan Pérez Jolote (Pozas), 161
Juárez, Benito, *37*, 76, 78, 79–80,
 82, 83

KENNEDY, President John F., 174

LAGUNA REGION, 24, 114, 131
land, legislation on ownership, 76;
 see also agrarian reform
landscape, 9, 13–31 *passim*
Latin American Free Trade
 Association, 171
Lerdo de Tejada, Miguel (*see*
 Who's Who, p. 195), 76
Lerdo de Tejada, Sebastian (*see*
 Who's Who, p. 195), 82, 86
Lewis, Oscar, 135–9
Ley Lerdo, 76, 89
liberals, Mexican, 69, 71, 72, 76–7,
 92
Limantour, José (*see* Who's Who,
 p. 195), 93, 97

Lind, John, 100
literature, 160–4
Lombardo Toledano, Vicente (*see*
  Who's Who, p. 195), 112, 154
López Mateos, Adolfo (*see* Who's
  Who, p. 195), 120, 175
López y Fuentes, Gregorio, 161
Los de Abajo (Azuela), 160
Lower California, 14, 21, 133

MADERO, Francisco (*see* Who's
  Who, p. 196), 93, 95–100, 101,
  103, 146
Madero, Gustavo, *38*, 99
Madrazo, Carlos, 157
Magia y Cybernetica, 163
Magón, Enrique and Ricardo, 93
Márquez, Gen. Leonardo, 77
Martínez, Gen. Mucio, 83
Maximilian, Archduke (*see* Who's
  Who, p. 196), *36*, *37*, 78, 79
Maya civilization, 29–31 *passim*,
  42*ff*., 159
Mejía, Gen., 79
Mendoza, Antonio de, 58
Mérida, 30
Mestizo cultural group, 11, 49, 51,
  52, 63, 64, 70, 71, 72, 80, 84, 92,
  158, 169
Mexican Eagle Oil Co., 88–9
Mexican Railway Co. Ltd., 86
Mexico and Its Heritage (Gruening),
  161
Mexico City 10, 14, 15, 16–17, 27,
  63–4, 75, 77, 78, 82, 86, 91, 99,
  102, *121*, *122*, *125*, 135, 137, 138,
  142, 179

Michoacán, 111
minerals, 62, 86, 104, 142; *see also*
  silver mining
Miramón, Gen. Miguel, 77, 79
miscegenation, *see Mestizo*
Moctezuma (*see* Who's Who,
  p. 196), 45, 55, 56
Monclava, 141
Monroe Doctrine, 78
Monterrey, 24, 137, 141, 142
Morelia, 21
Morelos, Fr. José María (*see* Who's
  Who, p. 196–7), 68–9, 72, 80, 89
Morelos, Vale of, 17, 18, 97, 99,
  102
Morfín, Efrain González, 154
Morones, Luis (*see* Who's Who,
  p. 197), 103, 106, 113
Morrow, Dwight, 109, 110
Múgica, Gen. Francisco, 103, 117
Murillo, Gerardo, *see* Atl, Dr

NACIONAL FINANCIERA
  development bank, 143
Napoleon Bonaparte, 67
Napoleon III, emperor, 78, 79
National Ejidal Bank, 114
National Railways of Mexico, 88
National Revolutionary Party,
  110, 111, 117–8
Netzahualcoatl, 46–7
Nicaragua, 173
Nicholson, Irene, 28
non-alignment, 170*ff*.

OAXACA (state and town), 25, 26,
  42, 58, 82, 83

Obregón, Alvaro (*see* Who's Who, p. 197), *39*, 101, 102–3, 106–9 *passim*, 131

O'Donojú, Juan, 69

oil industry, 27, 28, 88·9, 104, 107, 108, 109, 115–17, *123*, 141, 143, 172

opposition, political, to PRI, 153–4, 157

Organization of American States, 173–4

Orozco, José Clemente (*see* Who's Who, p. 197), 52, 107, 160

Orozco, Pascual, 96, 99

Ortiz Rubio, Pascual (*see* Who's Who, p. 197), 110

O'Shaughnessy, Hugh, 150

PALENQUE, 28, 29

Pan American Union, 173

Papaloapan Valley, 133

Paredes, Gen., 75

Partido Acción Nacional, 154

Partido Auténtica de la Revolución, 154

Partido de la Revolución Mexicana, *Partido Popular Socialista*, 154

Partido Revolucionario Institucional, 119, 148–54 *passim*, 157

'Pastry War' (1838), 74

Paz, Octavio (*see* Who's Who, p. 197), 158, 163–4

Peace by Revolution (Tannenbaum), 161

Pearson, S., and Co., 86–9

Pemex, 117, 141

peonage, 61–2, 90, 92, 93

Pershing, Gen. John J., 102

'Personalism' in Mexican politics, 72–3

Peru, 170

Plan Chontalpa, 30

Plan of Ayala, 98

Plan of Guadalupe, 101

Plan of Iguala, 69

Plan of San Luis Potosí, 96

PNR, *see* National Revolutionary Party

Polk, President James, K., 75

Portes Gil, Emilio (*see* Who's Who, p. 197), 110

positivism, 92, 158

Potrero No. 4 oil well, 88

Power and the Glory, The (Greene), 29

Pozas, Ricardo, 161

presidency, 71, 149–50

Presidential Succession of 1910 (Madero), 95

PRI, see *Partido Revolucionario Institucional*

PRM, *see* Partido de la Revolucion Mexicana

Puebla, 18–19, 137, 142; Battle of (1862), 78

Punta del Este Conference (1961), 174; (1962) 173

QUIROGA, Vasco de, 60

RAILWAY DEVELOPMENT under Díaz, 86–8

railway takeover by Cárdenas, 115

rainfall, 15

ranching, *see* cattle ranching
Raza Cosmica, La (Vasconcelos), 162
Redfield, Robert, 135
religion, Mexican, 42, 43–4, 46–7, 50–1; *see also* Roman Catholic Church
Région Más Transparente, La (Fuentes), 162–3
Renaissance, post-1910, 159*ff*
Repartimiento 59–60
Revolution (1810), 66–8; (1910), 52, 95–117 *passim*, 158–9
revolutionary parties, *see* National Revolutionary Party; Partido de la Revolución, Revolucionario
Reyes, Alfonso, 158
Reyes, Bernardo, 99
Rio Blanco Mills, civil disorders at, 93
Rivera, Diego (*see* Who's Who, p. 198), 10, 18, *40*, 52, 107, 160
Rodó, José Enrique, 163
Rodríguez, Gen. Abelardo (*see* Who's Who, p. 198), 110
Roman Catholic Church, 20, 48–9, 50–1, 54, 60–1, 64, 70, 71, 80, 84, 105, 108, 109, 113, 114, 135, 166–7; enforced sale of its estates, 76, 77
Roosevelt, President Franklin Delano, 116, 172
Ruiz Cortínez, Adolfo (*see* Who's Who, p. 198), 120

Sahagún, Bernardino de, 60

Salina Cruz, 27, 87
San Angel craft market, 164
San Luis Potosí, 77, 117
Sánchez family, 137–9, 168
Santa Anna, Gen. Antonio López de (*see* Who's Who, p. 198), 73, 74, 75
Scott, Gen. Winfield, 75
Seward, William Henry, 79
Sierra, Justo (*see* Who's Who, p. 198)
Sierra Madre, 13–14, 133
silver mining, 18, 27, 60, 62, 77
Simpson, Eyler N., 161
Sinaloa, 133
Sinarquismo, 162
Siqueiros, David Alfaro (*see* Who's Who, p. 198), 10, 52, 107, 160
socialism, 93, 103, 106, 107, 114, 158
Sonora, 101, 133
Spain, colonial government, 58–60; influence of, on Mexico, 11, 26, 45, 48–9, 50–2, 53–65 *passim*, 78, 162; Mexico's current relations with, 177
steel, 141
Stronge, Francis, 100
students, *127*, 155–7
Suarez, Pino, 100
sugar cultivation, 18, 25, 97, 133

Tabasco, 28–30, 109, 143
Tampico, 88; invasion (1829), 73
Tannenbaum, Frank, 161
Taxco, 18

Taylor, Gen. Zachary, 75
Tehuantepec Isthmus, 13, 27, 86–7
Tenochtitlán, 16, 44, 48
Teotihuacán, 20, 42, 43, 47
Tepozotlán, 20, *35*
Tepoztlán, 134–6
Terrazas, Luis, 90
Texas, 74
Tierra Caliente, 28*ff*.
Tlatelolco, College of, 60; market at, 47; riot (1968), 156; tower, *124*
Tlaxcalan people, 55
tobacco, 62
Toltec people, 43, 46, 47
Toluca, 21, 142
Torreón, 24
Torre, Haya de la, 170
Torres, Luis, 83
tourism, 9, 18, 25
trade, Aztec, 48; colonial, 62; late colonial, 67
trade unions, 93, 104
Trotsky, Leon, 177
Tula, 43, 44

UNITED NATIONS, 169, 175–6
United States, 24, 25, 64–5, 70, 74, 78, 79, 86, 87, 88, 96, 97, 98, 99, 100–1, 102, 107, 108, 109, 115–17, 118, 144, 161, 162, 163, 165, 169, 170, 171–8 *passim*
urbanization, 129–30, 136–9, 161, 165

VALLEY OF MEXICO, 15–16, 20, 30, 42, 43, 142
Vasconcelos, José (*see* Who's Who, p. 198–9), 107, 162
Velasco, President of Peru, 170
Vera Cruz (state and town), 20, 30, 73, 74, 75, 77, 78, 86, 87, 101, 143
Villa, Pancho (*see* Who's Who, p. 199), 25, *38–9*, 96, 101, 102, 103, 155, 160, 163

WAUGH, Evelyn, 116
wheat production, 133
Wilson, Henry Lane, 98, 99, 100
Wilson, President Woodrow, 100, 101, 102, 103
Wyke, Sir Charles, 78

YOUTH, 155–7
Yucatán Peninsula, 14, 29, 30, 73, 83

ZAPATA, Emiliano (*see* Who's Who, p. 199), 18, *39*, 97, 98–104 *passim*, 136, 155
Zapotec Kingdom, 42
Zea, Leopoldo, 163
Zócalo, 16
Zuloaga, Gen. Felix, 77
Zumárraga, Juan de, Bishop of Mexico, 60